DARK OF THE MOON

DARK
OF THE MOON

by

HOWARD RICHARDSON

and

WILLIAM BERNEY

Revised Edition

ROUTLEDGE/THEATRE ARTS BOOKS

NEW YORK

Published by
Routledge
Taylor & Francis Group
270 Madison Avenue
New York, NY 10016

Published in Great Britain by
Routledge
Taylor & Francis Group
2 Park Square
Milton Park, Abingdon
Oxon OX14 4RN

Routledge is an imprint of Taylor & Francis Group

Printed in the United States of America on acid-free paper

International Standard Book Number-10: 0-87830-517-3 (Softcover)
International Standard Book Number-13: 978-0-87830-517-9 (Softcover)

Library of Congress Cataloging-in-Publication Data

Catalog record is available from the Library of Congress

Taylor & Francis Group
is the Academic Division of T&F Informa plc.

Visit the Taylor & Francis Web site at
http://www.taylorandfrancis.com

and the Routledge Web site at
http://www.routledge-ny.com

FOREWORD TO THE NEW EDITION

My publisher has asked me to write an introduction to this new revised edition of "Dark of the Moon" and suggested that I put down how the play came to be. The creation of any work of literature is a unique process that defies analysis, and the genesis of a play of joint authorship is doubly difficult to dissect and explain. After a play is completed, the co-authors may look back and say, "This is how we did it," but in beginning their next play they often have to start from scratch and work out a new system. This is certainly true of the plays I wrote with William Berney.

I have written over forty plays with one person or another, counting my television dramas, so I suppose I am as well equipped as the next writer to discuss the problems of working with another playwright on a single project. But I find the question of how it is done almost impossible to answer—at least in general terms.

Although I suppose the truly great masterpieces of the theatre are the creations of the single artist, a collaboration offers certain distinct advantages both to the writers as well as others associated with the first production of the play. For one thing writing is essentially a lonely occupation, and for someone who enjoys the company of another person while he works, a co-author can make the process of play construction a companionable enterprise. Plays are composed essentially of the spoken word, and the drama that is orally conceived—much in the manner of "method" actors in an improvisational exercise—tends to have at least playable, natural dialogue on the credit side of its ledger.

But I believe the chief advantage of collaboration is that from its very conception the work is not "my play" but "our play." When any play is first produced, the writer must eventually come to think in terms of a communal project, and the sooner he can accept this concept of joint responsibility with his producer, direc-

tor, designer, and cast, the better his chances for a successful production. It is my experience that co-authors are not nearly so
difficult to work with as is the playwright who thinks of his
"brain child" as his sole property, something to be jealously
guarded and protected at all cost from those who are out to
destroy it by changing lines. Actually the only disadvantage of
co-authorship I can think of is that the royalties have to be divided.

The Russian ballerina, Pavlova, was once asked how long it
took her to learn to dance. "Not very long," she replied, "just
all my life." I am often tempted to give the same reply when
asked how long it took to write "Dark of the Moon." The history
of this play is in a true sense the story of my life—and I can
hardly be expected to attempt an autobiography in the next few
paragraphs.

The actual writing of the first draft was accomplished in two
weeks during my Christmas vacation in 1941, when I decided
not to go home to North Carolina but instead stay to work on
a play, which was the assignment in a writing class I was taking
at the State University of Iowa. "Night Song" was what I called
it then and that was the name under which it was first copy-
righted. That summer it was produced at the University Theatre
under the title, "Barbara Allen," and shortly after that it won the
Maxwell Anderson Award, given by Stanford University for the
best verse drama of the year. The award consisted of the honor
and one hundred dollars.

By this time we were at war and I was in the army, waiting
to be called to active duty as an aviation cadet. I decided to spend
my award money, plus a little I had saved, on a trip to New York
City to try my chances at Broadway. I remembered the advice
my uncle, Thomas Dixon, had once given me. "If you want to
kiss the girls at the Sunday school picnic, you first have to go to
the Sunday school picnic. There's no guarantee that you'll kiss
'em if you go, but you can be sure you won't if you don't." It
was advice he himself had followed. He was one of the first
writers to go out to Hollywood in 1916 where he wrote the
screen play for "A Birth of a Nation." Although Uncle Tom died

destitute and a ward of the state of North Carolina, his picnic had been a long and a merry one. For the young playwright in 1941, as it is today, the picnic grounds of the theatre are in New York. He has not made it until he has made it on Broadway.

Upon arriving in the city, my first task was to locate Maxwell Anderson, who I naturally assumed would welcome with open arms his prize-winning protegé. Although I did meet the eminent playwright briefly and left with him a copy of my play, as far as I know he never read it. Certainly I never heard from him again. My only other contact was a letter of introduction to Amos Basel, a lawyer, who had once represented Hartsel Spence, the Iowa novelist. Mr. Basel is now a judge in the Criminal Court of New York City, but at that time he was the law partner of Miss Rebecca Brownstein, the attorney for Actors Equity, and through her had many theatrical contacts. I was to learn later that these contacts were mostly the result of lawsuits that the actors' union brought against managements. Miss Brownstein is a lawyer of formidable ability in and out of a courtroom and she usually wins her clients' cases. Mr. Basel and Miss Brownstein liked my play and I signed a contract with them to be my agents.

I read in a newspaper that José Ferrer and his wife, Uta Hagen, were looking for a new play to star in. They had both recently come into prominence and were hailed as the Lunt-Fontanne team of their generation. With this in mind, I left a copy of my manuscript backstage at the theatre where they were playing in an easily-forgotten comedy called "Niki." Within three days Mr. Ferrer telephoned me. He wanted to produce my play himself with his wife as his co-star—and would I spend the week-end with them in their home in Ossining? I was now an established playwright with agents, stars, and a producer!

It was then that I first learned the true meaning of the adage, "Plays are not written but rewritten." I began a series of revisions and changes that has continued down to the present day. I was busily at work on my third draft, when the call to arms sent me off into the wild blue yonder. I turned the responsibility for any further work on the play over to my friend, William

Berney, who had been at Iowa with me when it was first produced—and so our collaboration began.

I don't want to give the impression in any way of belittling Bill's contribution to "Dark of the Moon." He was a Southerner and a poet with a keen ear for rural, folk, idiomatic speech, and a flair for the dramatic. Some of the best lines in the play as well as its final title were supplied by him. I doubt that the play would ever have reached Broadway but for him.

In due time, Mr. Ferrer and Miss Hagen went their separate ways, the option was dropped, and the war went on.

During the next three years "Dark of the Moon" was read and rejected by every established Broadway producer. The Theatre Guild long considered doing it, but finally decided that instead they would produce a musical adaptation of a play by Lynn Riggs, which they were calling "Away We Go." I would like to think that they made a tragic mistake, but in the light of history such a judgment would be hard to substantiate. The name of their musical was changed to "Oklahoma!"

By 1944 I was stationed in New York City and Bill was working for an advertising agency that handled the Boeing Aircraft account. I had long since come to a mutual understanding with the Army that if the war was to be won, I had best give up hope of becoming a fighter pilot. "You are a danger not only to yourself but to government property" was the way my flight instructor put it. Anyone who has ever taken a ride with me in my car will bear him out.

I remember one spring afternoon standing on the corner of Forty-fourth Street and Broadway after a particularly discouraging session with my agents and saying to myself, "Well, let's face up to it. The play will never get on Broadway. It's about time, Howard, you gave up." That night I received a telephone call from a young actor, Henry Barnard, who had given a copy of the script to his summer stock director, Robert Perry. Mr. Perry let his producer, John Huntington, read it. Mr. Huntington liked it and wanted to give it a try-out production in Brattle Hall, his theatre in Cambridge, Massachusetts. Brattle Hall was not the

Empire Theatre, nor was Cambridge Broadway, but Bill and I decided that we had little to lose. Bill through his agency was influential in letting *Life* magazine have exclusive first pictures of the new Boeing bomber, the B-29. In exchange, some people at *Life* promised that if our play was a success, they would try to cover it in the magazine.

"Dark of the Moon" opened that summer with Carol Stone and Richard Hart in the leading roles. We got our *Life* spread. The very producers who had previously turned it down now bid against each other for the right to present it on Broadway. We chose Lee and J. J. Shubert, since they guaranteed us a theatre at a time when that was a major problem on Broadway. We opened at the Forty-sixth Street Theatre in the spring of 1945, ran through the summer and into the next season, and then went on an extended road tour.

"Dark of the Moon" has by now played in most of the leading theatre capitals of the world, including London, Rome, Sydney, Johannesburg, and even Leningrad—though from this last production I have yet to receive so much as a kopeck. It has three times been produced on national television and has also become a favorite in amateur and college theatres and in high school auditoriums. Now there is hardly a night when it is not playing somewhere.

I have so many associations with this play—happy, humorous, tragic. My close friends, Bill Berney and Dick Hart, both of the Shubert brothers and most of the old character actors who worked with me in the early productions are now dead. During our run on Broadway one of our actors died in the wings during a performance and another had a heart attack in the revival scene and had to be carried off stage by the other actors as part of the action. In fact the death rate among the cast was so high, the actors began to believe the play was cursed. A petition was circulated among them demanding that the actual Bible used in the church be replaced. Their wish was granted, but the night that Preacher Haggler received his inspiration from Gray's *Anatomy* was the night the closing notice was posted back stage.

But "Dark of the Moon" has also been very lucky for many of those who have been connected with it. Such performers as Shelly Berman, Betsy Palmer, Paul Newman, and Marge Champion have played in it at one time or another before they became stars. Two leading directors, Ella Gerber and Peter Brook, were first brought into prominence by their productions of this play. Most of my closest friends are those who have been involved with me in this adventure, and happily we seem to be permanently tied to each other because of it.

I often wonder what my life might have been like had I decided to spend that Christmas at home.

Howard Richardson
New York City
Spring, 1966

THE BALLAD OF BARBARA ALLEN

A witch-boy from the mountain came,
A-pinin' to be human,
Fer he had seen the fairest gal . . .
A gal named Barbara Allen.

O Conjur Man, O Conjur Man,
Please do this thing I'm wantin'
Please change me to a human man,
Fer Barbara I'd be courtin'.

Now, Barbara had a red, red dress
And one she had of blue,
And many men did Barbara love,
But never was she true.

Oh, you can be a man, a man,
If Barbara will not grieve you,
If she be faithful fer a year,
Yer eagle, he will leave you.

O Barbara, will you marry me,
And will you leave me never,
Oh, yes, my love, I'll marry you,
And live with you ferever.

Words and music of the songs from Dark of the Moon *will be found at the end of the play.*

Dark of the Moon was first presented at the 46th Street Theatre, New York City, on 14th March 1945, by Messrs. Shubert, with the following cast:

JOHN	Richard Hart
CONJUR MAN	Ross Matthew
THE DARK WITCH	Iris Whitney
THE FAIR WITCH	Marjorie Belle
CONJUR WOMAN	Georgia Simmons
HANK GUDGER	John Gerstad
MISS METCALF	Frances Goforth
UNCLE SMELICUE	Roy Fant
MRS. SUMMEY	Kathryn Cameron
EDNA SUMMEY	Millicent Coleman
MR. ATKINS	James Lanphier
MRS. BERGER	Agnes Scott Yost
BURT DINWITTY	Robert Pryor
HATTIE HEFFNER	Peggy Ann Holmes
MR. BERGEN	Allan Tower
MR. SUMMEY	Gar Moore
MARVIN HUDGENS	John Gifford
BARBARA ALLEN	Carol Stone
FLOYD ALLEN	Conrad Janis
MRS. ALLEN	Maidel Turner
MR. ALLEN	Joseph Garry
PREACHER HAGGLER	Winfield Hoeny
GREENY GORMAN	Frances Brandt
OTHER WITCHES	Saralee Wimmer
	Jinx Heffelfinger
	Peggy Ann Holmes
	Lil Liandre

The Play Directed by
ROBERT E. PERRY

Production Designed and Lighted by
GEORGE JENKINS

Dances and Special Staging by
ESTHER JUNGER

CHARACTERS

JOHN

CON JUR MAN

DARK WITCH

FAIR WITCH

CON JUR WOMAN

HANK GUDGER

EDNA SUMMEY

MR. SUMMEY

MRS. SUMMEY

MISS METCALF

MR. ATKINS

MR. JENKINS

UNCLE SMELICUE

FLOYD ALLEN

MR. BERGEN

MRS. BERGEN

BURT DINWITTY

GREENY GORMAN

HATTIE HEFFNER

MARVIN HUDGENS

BARBARA ALLEN

MRS. ALLEN

MR. ALLEN

ELLA BERGEN

PREACHER HAGGLER

ACT ONE

ACT TWO

ACT ONE

Scene I

The scene is at the peak of a ridge in the Smoky Mountains. From the darkness can be seen the silhouette of a large tree rising gnarled and twisted against a windswept, cloudy sky. Offstage is heard the voice of a young man calling.

JOHN (*softly at first*): Conjur Man. (*Then louder*) Is you here, Conjur Man?

(*Over the top of the crag he emerges from the blackness.*)
Conjur Man!

CONJUR MAN (*from the darkness below*): Who that?

JOHN (*starting to climb down the rock*): Hit jes' me, Conjur Man.

CONJUR MAN (*closer but still unseen*): What me?

JOHN: John.

CONJUR MAN (*coming into view. He is as old and broken as the tree*): What you doin' here, witch boy? You ain't got no cause fer a-strayin'.

JOHN: But I got to see you, Conjur Man. I got to ast you somethin'.

CONJUR MAN: You got nothin' to ast me that you don't know the answer.

JOHN: I come a long way to see you and that ain't no way to treat me.

CONJUR MAN: How fur you come don't differ. Hit still no.

JOHN: Listen to me, Conjur Man. If you do this thing I ast, I swear I pay you anythin' you want. Make me into a human!

CONJUR MAN: Whar yer eagle, witch boy, yer eagle you been ridin'?

JOHN: Don't call me witch boy. My name John.

CONJUR MAN: John er witch don't make no never mind. You left yer eagle on Old Baldy?

I

JOHN: I walked here. I kin walk like anybody.

CONJUR MAN: Like anybody not a witch, I reckon's what you mean.

JOHN: Like anybody, witch er no witch.

CONJUR MAN: Yer eagle must be lonesome up on Old Baldy— alone on Old Baldy. Hit dark, and hit black.

JOHN: He kin git along without me. He'll have to larn to anyway.

CONJUR MAN: And kin you larn hit too, witch boy, larn to git along without eagles and sech? Hit mighty hard a-walkin', walkin' all the time, with no way to fly.

JOHN (*coming off the rock to the ground*): But hit don't differ, Conjur Man, not to them hit don't. Not to them what's never flied.

CONJUR MAN: But you ain't like them, witch boy. You ain't like the valley people.

JOHN: Thar ain't so much difference atween us.

CONJUR MAN: Thar more difference than you know. They got souls and go to heaven. They gits born, and live and die.

JOHN: I was born too, Conjur Man. And I'm gonna die.

CONJUR MAN: No, you ain't gonna die, witch boy. You jes' like all the other witches. You git jes' three hundred years, and then you nothin' but mountain fog.

JOHN: I ain't like other witches. I done lots a things that's human.

CONJUR MAN: What things, witch boy?

JOHN: Things like—lovin'.

CONJUR MAN: But yer pappy was a buzzard, and yer maw was a witch.

JOHN: Hit don't make no never mind. You could change me, Conjur Man. You say yerself you could change me like them others, like them others in the valley, them with souls that go to heaven.

CONJUR MAN: But what fer you want to, witch boy? You don't know the thing you ast. Hit ain't easy bein' human. Hit jes' workin' all the time, workin' in the field with a mule and a plow.

JOHN: I know what hit like. I seen 'em. Workin' ain't so hard. And thar's dancin', and thar's guitars, and thar's singin' in the church.

CONJUR MAN: What you doin' in the church, boy? You a witch, and that one place whar you ain't allowed.

JOHN: I jes' stood thar at the winder lookin' at the folks inside. Ain't no harm in standin' watchin'. 'Tain't no harm in that.

CONJUR MAN: You keep away from that thar church, boy. 'Tain't no place fer witches to hang around. Even if I made you human, that one place you couldn't never go.

JOHN: I could go thar if I wanted. I could go be sanctified.

CONJUR MAN: Witch boy, listen at me talkin'. Witches can't be changed completely. Thar's allus somethin' 'bout the witch they wunst was that's left inside 'em. That thar somethin' can't be changed. Hit lies sleepin' thar inside 'em, sleepin' and a-dreamin' a the days he was a witch, dreamin' a the nights he rode a-screamin' and a-cryin' 'gainst the blackness a the sky. And thar jes' one thing that wake him, and that the Lord Gawd Jesus.

(THE DARK WITCH *appears on the top of the rock.*)

JOHN: I ain't skeerd a no Gawd Jesus. I ain't got no truck with him.

(THE FAIR WITCH *appears on another crag, and the two witches laugh derisively.*)

What you doin' here?

DARK WITCH: Jes' watchin'.

JOHN: This ain't got nothin' to do with you. Listen at me, Conjur Man, if you do this thing I ast you, if you make me into jes' a plain man——

FAIR WITCH: You want to leave us, witch boy? You tired a the moonlight?

CONJUR MAN: I done said no wunst and I say hit again. (*Move*) Now leave me be, and don't come messin' 'round here more. You a witch and a witch you'll stay.

CONJUR WOMAN (*offstage*): What that out thar, Conjur Man? Who that out thar with you makin' all that fuss?

CONJUR MAN: Hit jes' John the witch boy.

CONJUR WOMAN (*coming into view*): What he want?

DARK WITCH: He been astin' Conjur Man to change him.

FAIR WITCH: He tired a bein' a witch.

JOHN: I want to be a human. I been astin' and a-astin', but he still say no.

CONJUR WOMAN: You ain't ast me yit.

CONJUR MAN: Old lady, I'm a-tellin' you. Don't start no truck with witches.

CONJUR WOMAN: You ain't ast me, witch boy.

JOHN: Would you do hit, Conjur Woman?

CONJUR WOMAN: I might could be persuaded. I might could be persuaded, but hit mighty hard to do.

CONJUR MAN: Now ole lady——

CONJUR WOMAN: Hesh yer talkin'.

CONJUR MAN (*starting offstage*): Don't say I didn't warn you, witch boy. Bein' human ain't so easy as ridin' on the night.

(*He is swallowed in the darkness. There is a peal of thunder.*)

JOHN: You really meant hit, what you said about me bein' human? You warn't jes' sayin' things to edge me on?

CONJUR WOMAN: Witch boy, tell me somethin'. Have you ever been in love?

FAIR WITCH: I reckon he has, Conjur Woman.

CONJUR WOMAN: I don't mean in love with witches.

(THE DARK WITCH *laughs scornfully.*)

No, I mean with someone human.

JOHN: Human. Yeah, she's human.

CONJUR WOMAN: So that the real reason. Hit's hard to go a-courtin' a gal when you a witch.

JOHN: That ain't the only reason, but I reckon hit the main one.

CONJUR WOMAN: And what the gal's name, witch boy John?

JOHN: Her name Barbara. Barbara Allen. Blue-eyed Barbara Allen with the copper hair.

CONJUR WOMAN (*laughing ribaldly*): She's jes' the gal fer you to be a-courtin'!

JOHN: But I love her, Conjur Woman. The first time I seed her she were climbin' up the mounting—up Hangin' Dawg Mountting—and the sun were in her hair. I were on my eagle, and I sailed low fer to see her. She look up kinda skeerd like, but then she smiled and waved. I knowed I hadn't oughter, that witchin' is fer night time, but she the purtiest gal I reckon that thar is.

DARK WITCH: She ain't purty. Hit jes' you that think so.

CONJUR WOMAN: That right. She ain't purty.

JOHN: She purty all right. I 'low I should know. I kissed her.

(THE WITCHES *and the* CONJUR WOMAN *laugh.*)

CONJUR WOMAN: A witch boy kissin' a gal what's human! And that warn't the only thing you done.

JOHN: I reckon not. Not a ward we said atween us, but hit warn't no time fer talkin'. The sun were in her hair. Her hair was golden and a-shinin' as hit twisted through my fingers, but hit were black against the starlight afore I let her go.

DARK WITCH: You'll be sorry, witch boy.

(*She disappears over the rock.*)

FAIR WITCH: You'll be sorry.

(*She too disappears.*)

CONJUR WOMAN: Witch boy, I know more 'bout this than you'll ever know.

JOHN: What you know that I don't?

CONJUR WOMAN: I know that Barbara Allen's gonna birth yer child.

(*There is a rumble of thunder.*)

JOHN: What you mean?

CONJUR WOMAN (*laughing*): Barbara Allen's gonna birth yer child.

JOHN: Then you gotta make me human. I'll do anything you ast me.

CONJUR WOMAN: What about them witch gals? They might make trouble.

JOHN: Hit don't differ with me.

CONJUR WOMAN: I think you need some larnin', witch boy, you need to larn a lesson. So I'll give you yer wish. But you got to promise somethin'.

JOHN: Anythin' you ast me.

CONJUR WOMAN: You got to make Barbara Allen yer wife.

(*There is another peal of thunder.*)

JOHN: Is that all I gotta promise?

CONJUR WOMAN: That all.

JOHN: Jes' that I'll git married to Barbara?

CONJUR WOMAN: That all you got to promise and you git the thing you wants.

JOHN (*leaping back up on the rock*): Then I'll be a human. No more ridin' with my eagle, black against the moonlight, a streak against the sky. No more diggin' in the graveyard, no more yellin' in the night and a-screamin' with a long high cry that splashes 'gainst the stars!

CONJUR WOMAN: You won't miss doin' that, will you, witch boy?

JOHN: I reckon not, Conjur Woman.

CONJUR WOMAN: But yer eagle, he'll still be thar waitin' fer you —waitin' and a-longing' fer the night when you come back. You'll miss the moonlight. As long as you're a human you'll never see the moon. You'll git so sick and tired of earth.

JOHN: That time'll never come. I kin live without a moon.

CONJUR WOMAN: Perhaps and then perhaps not. We'll see.

(*She starts offstage.*)

JOHN: But you'll change me fer allus, won't you? Wunst you're a human thar ain't no turnin' back.

CONJUR WOMAN: That depend on Barbara Allen.

JOHN: What you meanin' by that, Conjur Woman?

CONJUR WOMAN: I mean she gotta be true to you, boy, faithful fer a year. Wunst you're married, wunst you're her husband, if that gal go off with another man, you'll find yer eagle flyin' down from Baldy, flyin' with the moonlight, fer you'll be a witch agin!

JOHN: She shore a purty gal—Barbara.

CONJUR WOMAN: Are you ready, witch boy, ready fer the changin'?

JOHN: I reckon, Conjur Woman.

CONJUR WOMAN: Hit ain't easy changin' witches. Hit the hardest thing I know. Hit takes spider webs and graveyard dirt, and a ring from the finger of a cold, dead hand.

JOHN: I kin git 'em, Conjur Woman. I know whar I kin find 'em. I'll git 'em and you'll change me, and I'll be a witch no more!

(*There is a flash of lightning, accompanied by a crack of thunder, and as the lightning fades, the stage goes back with it. Thunder continues in the distance.*)

Scene II

The scene is the central square of Buck Creek. It has been roped off for the weekly Saturday night dance. Lanterns have been swung, and they give a festive note to the setting. There are several groups of early arrivals, laughing and exchanging greetings. On a raised platform the band, consisting of UNCLE SMELICUE *with his guitar and an accordion player, is tuning up. Snatches of conversation can be heard, and the group joins in from time to time on the song which* MR. JENKINS *leads off. Among the crowd several girls vie with each other in bits of dancing, and here and there a flirtation is pantomimed.*

JENKINS (*sings*):
> Thar ain't no gal like a mountain gal,
> At night she's yore honey and by day yore pal,
> Do all yer work if you sing the right tune,
> And dance yore feet off by the light a the moon.

GROUP:

> Smoky Mountain gal won't do me no harm,
> I love her and trust her as fur as the barn.

ATKINS:

> A mountain gal is jes' like the breeze—
> She's fast in the valley, but caught whar thar's trees,
> Spend all yer money till you lose yer mind.
> Tell you that she love you and leave you behind.

GROUP:

> Smoky Mountain gal, etc.

EDNA:

> I got me a cabin, I got me a cow,
> Ain't never been married, but I know how.

SMELICUE:

> Little Mountain gal, won't you come out with me,
> Thar's a side a myself that I want you to see.

GROUP:

> Smoky Mountain gal, etc.

(*The song ends in a burst of merriment.*)

HANK (*as* MISS METCALF *comes out of the general store*): Howdy, Miss Metcalf. Glad to see you out.

MISS METCALF: Howdy.

(*She crosses to shake hands with* JENKINS.)

JENKINS: Hit the damp weather I reckon that's been keepin' you a-beddin' hit.

MISS METCALF: I reckon, Mr. Jenkins, and hit look like rain to-night.

(*There's a flash of lightning.*)

SMELICUE: Well, I declare afore goodness, Miz Summey. Hain't seed you sinst dogwood bloomin' time.

MRS. SUMMEY (*coming over to him*): Well, hain't been stirrin' about much. Feel kinda puny.

SMELICUE: You lookin' well.

MRS. SUMMEY: Well, I don't feel so well. Ain't felt right smart fer nigh on two year.

ELLA (*coming on stage*): Howdy, Floyd Allen. Is thar room fer me on the wagon?

FLOYD: I reckon. Ain't you gonna do no dancin'?

ELLA: No, I'm jes' a-settin' to-night.

(*There is a rumble of thunder.*)

ATKINS: Gawd, listen to that thunder! Hit's be a plumb shame iffen we can't have the dance.

HANK: Hit'd be a shame aright, and that a fact.

MRS. BERGEN: Howdy, Uncle Smelicue. You lookin' spry. Heerd tell as how you was tuckered up with rheumatism.

SMELICUE: My rheumatism's kinda calmed down sinst I been totin' them horse chestnuts around in my pocket.

MRS. BERGEN: Is that a fact?

SMELICUE: A fact afore Gawd. Hope this here storm don't start hit up agin.

(*There is a flash of lightning, followed by thunder.*)

EDNA: Hit ain't a goin' to storm. I kin tell hit by the sky. That jes' heat lightnin'.

ATKINS: But heat lightnin' don't thunder. Don't thunder, I tell you. Hit ain't no natural night fer a dance.

MRS. BERGEN: You right thar, Mr. Atkins. Like I said to my husband, hit more like a night fer witches to fly.

MR. BERGEN: Don't you go startin' on that, Gabby Bergen. That ain'st no way fer a Christian to talk.

MRS. BERGEN: That the way I feel about hit. Why Greeny Gorman! Whar you been?

(*She goes over to* GREENY.)

GREENY: Been over to Coon Holler for a fortnight.

MR. BERGEN: How's the young uns over thar?

MR. SUMMEY (*going over to* SMELICUE): How are you, Uncle Smelicue? Heerd yer cousin Emmer married a right well-to-do man.

(BARBARA *and* MARVIN *come in, greeting those they meet.*)

SMELICUE: Mebbe so; but she still milkin' cows and totin' manure to the field.

MARVIN: You shore is purty to-night, Miss Barbara. You shore is purty in that dress.

BARBARA: I'm glad you like hit, Marvin Hudgens. Hit were a gift from a friend I know.

MARVIN: You ain't tuck no clothes off that Rome Agar?

BARBARA: I might could be.

MARVIN: Don't you be lettin' that man mess with you.

BARBARA: But Rome Agar is a friend of mine. 'Sides, I didn't say hit were him, did I?

(*She laughs, teasing him, and tosses her scarf at him.*)

FLOYD: Hit nigh ready for the dancin'.

MISS METCALF: Hit a plumb shame thar ain't more folks.

JENKINS: I reckon hit the storm that's keepin' 'em off.

MISS METCALF: I reckon.

MR. SUMMEY: Let's have a song afore we start.

GROUP:
    Yes, let's have a song. Let's have a song from Barbara Allen. A song, Barbara. Sing us a song.

MISS METCALF (*coming down to* BARBARA): Sing us your song, the one about Barbara and the witch boy.

BARBARA: But that's a sad song. I allus like the gay ones best.

JENKINS: But hit a purty song, Barbara Allen.

ATKINS: I reckon hit about as purty a song as I know.

MISS METCALF: Hit allus makes me want to cry.

BARBARA: Well, hit don't me. Any gal what can't take care a herself has hit comin' to her, I say.

EDNA: I reckon you have, Barbara Allen.

BARBARA: But I kin take care a myself, Edna Summey. I kin take care a myself right fine.

EDNA: But you ain't got a husband, a man fer to marry you. You ain't got no feller to make you he bride.

MRS. SUMMEY: Hesh yer mouth, Edna Summey.

EDNA: But Maw, hit the truth.

MRS. SUMMEY: I'm a-talkin'. You ain't got no cause fer to say things like that.

EDNA: Aw, lemme alone.

MRS. SUMMEY: Barbara git married when she a-ready.

EDNA: But hit better be soon, Maw. Hit better be soon.

(BARBARA *starts towards* EDNA, *but* MR. JENKINS *stops her just as* HANK *and* MRS. SUMMEY *pull* EDNA *back.*)

BURT: Floyd Allen, you gonna let that gal talk about yore sister like that?

FLOYD: I can't hep hit if what she say is true.

EDNA: She better git married quick.

BARBARA: I'll git married when I got a mind to. I kin name me the man, the time, and the place. You kin come to the weddin'.

EDNA: I reckon I ain't got that long fer to live. You kin pleasure yerself every night if you want to, pleasure yerself on a sweet potato bank, but that ain't no sign that the man's fer to marry you.

(HANK *pats her shoulder approvingly.*)

BARBARA: I reckon hit might could be, Edna Summey.

EDNA: Well, hit better be quick afore you're disgraced. Afore you're disgraced by beddin' a bastard.

(BARBARA *flies at her and the two start hairpulling.* MARVIN, JENKINS, HANK *and* MRS. SUMMEY *separate them.*)

MRS. SUMMEY: Shet yer face, Edna Summey.

(*She slaps* EDNA.)

EDNA: Maw! That hurt!

MRS. SUMMEY: That's jes' a start of what you'll git if you don't mind yer tongue.

EDNA: But Maw, hit the truth. Why, everybody know the truth about Barbara Allen.

MRS. SUMMEY: This here a dance you at, Edna Summey, so you mind yer manners when you talk.

MISS METCALF: Ain't you gonna sing us the song, Barbara?

GROUP: Yes, sing us the song, Barbara.

SMELICUE: You sing fer us and I'll dance at yer weddin' in the hog trough.

EDNA: She can't sing nohow, can't sing fer sour apples.

BARBARA: Is that so? Well, I guess I kin. Come on, Uncle Smelicue. I'll sing.

(SMELICUE *strums a chord or two and* BARBARA *sings.*)

> A witch boy from the mountain came,
> A-pinin' to be human,
> Fer he had seen the fairest gal—
> A gal named Barbara Allen.
> O Conjur Man, O Conjur Man,
> Please do this thing I'm wantin'—
> Please change me to a human man,
> Fer Barbara I'd be courtin'.
> Now Barbara had a red, red dress.
> And one she had of blue,
> And many men did Barbara love,
> But never was she true.
> Oh, you can be a man, a man
> If Barbara will not grieve you,
> If she be faithful fer a year,
> Yer eagle, he will leave you.

(JOHN *comes onstage, unnoticed by the crowd, and watches her.*)

> O Barbara, will you marry me,
> And will you leave me never?

(JOHN *moves closer to her, still unnoticed.*)

(*She suddenly stops singing, and* SMELICUE'S *accompaniment dies away.*)

MR. SUMMEY (*after a pause*): What the matter, Barbara Allen?

BARBARA: Nothin'.

(MARVIN, *then several others in the crowd, suddenly turn to look at* JOHN, *whose eyes are glued to* BARBARA.)

MR. BERGEN: Go on, sing it, Barbara.

BARBARA: I don't wanta.

SMELICUE: Hit bad luck not to finish a song.

BARBARA: I fergit hit. I can't remember the endin'. (*She turns slowly until she is looking at* JOHN.) Let's dance.

ATKINS: Yes, let's start the dancin', everybody.

OTHERS: Yes, let's begin.

SMELICUE: Git yore partners, everybody. All jine hands and here we go!

(*The group falls silent as* JOHN *walks slowly up to* BARBARA, *whose hands* MARVIN *is holding.*)

JOHN: Kin I be yore partner?

MARVIN: Barbara Allen's dancin' with me.

JOHN: Kin I be yore partner, Barbara Allen?

MARVIN: You heerd what I said.

JOHN: But I didn't ast you.

MARVIN: I reckon you don't know who you a-talkin' to.

JOHN: I reckon I don't, and I don't much care.

MARVIN: I'm Marvin Hudgens.

JOHN (*his eyes still on* BARBARA): Glad to meet you.

MARVIN: Ain't you never heerd a me?

JOHN: Can't say as I have, *Mister* Hudgens.

MARVIN: I'm the strongest man in this here county.

(*Ad lib by* GROUP.)

Thar ain't a man in this county can rassle with me.

JOHN (*facing him*): But I ain't from this county, Marvin Hudgens. I ain't from this county, so that don't include me.

MARVIN: Then I reckon you astin' fer trouble.

JOHN: I could be.

MARVIN: Well, you come to the right place to find hit. I'm a-tellin' you, Barbara's my gal and she dancin' with me.

JOHN: Barbara ain't no gal a yourn.

MARVIN: I ain't aimin' to start no trouble, but you'll take that back afore you done.

JOHN: I might could be, Marvin Hudgens. I might could be, and I might not.

MARVIN: I'm a-waitin' fer you to take back what you said about Barbara.

JOHN: Barbara ain't no gal a yourn.

MISS METCALF: Now this here a dance, and we don't want no trouble.

JOHN: I ain't asting fer trouble. I'm astin' to dance.

MARVIN: Well, this here one dance whar you ain't wanted, so git on out and leave us be.

JOHN: I'm a-stayin' right here and I'm a-dancin', and I'm a-dancin' with Barbara Allen.

MARVIN: I'll give you three to git you gone. I'll give you three and then I'll whop you—whop you so hard you'll think the lightnin' struck you.

(*There is a flash of lightning, followed by thunder, and the crowd laughs.*)

JOHN: I'm a-waitin' fer you, Marvin Hudgens.

MARVIN: ONE!

MR. SUMMEY: You think he'll stay.

MISS METCALF: He look a powerful man.

MR. SUMMEY: But he don't know Marvin.

JOHN: I'm a-waitin'.

MARVIN: TWO!

MRS. BERGEN: This here are better'n the county fair.

MISS METCALF: But I feel right sorry for the stranger.

BARBARA: He kin take care a hisself, I reckon.

JOHN: Much obliged. I reckon as how I kin.

MARVIN: Well, are you goin', or is it trouble you're wantin'?

JOHN: You ain't fergot what come after two?

MARVIN: You black-bellied mule mouth, I'll manage you proper. Gimme room, boys, the number is three!

(*He backs up, then rushes at* JOHN. *As he raises his arm* JOHN *touches it and there is a brilliant flash of lightning. As it fades,* MARVIN *has fallen, and starts dazedly to get up.*)

JENKINS: Why, he didn't hardly tetch him!

BURT: Git up thar, Marvin. Git up and show him who you are.

MR. BERGEN: What the matter, Marvin Hudgens?

EDNA: Stranger jes' too stout, I reckon.

MISS METCALF: Why, he didn't whop him at all!

JOHN: I'm a-waitin' fer you, Marvin Hudgens. I'm a-waitin' fer yer promise.

MARVIN: You don't rassle fair.

(He staggers to his feet.)

JOHN: I rassle my way, you kin rassle yours.

BURT: You ain't gonna let him take yer gal, are you, Marvin? Why don't you pop him one in the haid?

MARVIN: I'm gittin' out a here.

BURT: But the dance ain't started yit.

MARVIN *(shoving him away)*: I ain't figgerin' on dancin'.

(He pushes his way through the crowd and exits.)

MR. BERGEN: Don't know as we can have the dance or not.

MISS METCALF: No need to start dancin', if hit goin' to rain right off.

MR. BERGEN: It has got real dark. Thar a storm a-comin' shore.

(JOHN is walking slowly toward BARBARA.)

EDNA: The clouds is mean and black-like. This ain't no night fer dancin'.

ATKINS: Hit jes' like the night Agnes Riddle were kilt.

HANK: Hit the Gawd's truth, Mr. Atkins. Hit were plumb like this. The clouds was low on the mounting, and a hoot owl was a-screechin'.

(JOHN has reached BARBARA, and lifts his hand to stroke her hair.)

MRS. BERGEN: Hit shore are a night fer witches to fly.

MISS METCALF: Don't talk about hit. Hit make me feel quare.

ATKINS: Let's start the dancin'.

OTHERS: Yes, let's begin, etc.

(The GROUP makes partners, BARBARA and JOHN dancing together, and the dance gets under way with SMELICUE and the accordion player providing square dance music. After several figures there is another flash of lightning and the GROUP stops, BARBARA clutching JOHN in sudden fright.)

MISS METCALF: Hit startin' to rain!

(*Some of the dancers stop, some go on dancing during the following.* JOHN, *holding* BARBARA, *slowly begins to whirl her around.*)

ATKINS: I knowed that warn't jes' heat lightnin'.

MR. BERGEN: Hit too bad to spile the dancin'. Maybe hit'll stop in a little while.

MRS. SUMMEY: Hit in fer a storm.

MR. SUMMEY: Come on, Maw. Let's git into the store. Edna, hurry up.

(*In a few minutes they have all left.* BARBARA *and* JOHN *dance alone for a minute, then* BARBARA *stops.*)

BARBARA: Why is all the others goin'?

JOHN: I reckon they think hit a-rainin'.

BARBARA: But hit ain't a-rainin'—not on us. I ain't even wet a bit.

JOHN: That cause you and me was dancin'.

(*He begins to dance, but stops when she doesn't follow.*)

BARBARA: I reckon I don't even know yore name.

JOHN: But we met afore, Barbara Allen. The night the wind came up and the moon went dark. Remember?

BARBARA: I remember. And thar ain't no moon to-night.

JOHN: And thar a wind. (*Pause.*) My name John.

BARBARA: John what?

JOHN: Jes' John.

BARBARA: John all right. Jes' like the ballad.

JOHN: I reckon I don't know that.

BARBARA: Hit jes' a song. Song I was singin'.

JOHN: But you stopped.

BARBARA: Hit a sad song. I like the gay ones best.

JOHN: Hit don't have to be sad. You never know the endin' till hit sung plumb through.

BARBARA: Then we'll make hit a gay one, and sing our own endin'.

(*She takes his hand.*)

JOHN: I reckon you crazy, Barbara Allen.

BARBARA: I reckon. Let's dance.

JOHN: We'll dance faster than the lightnin', faster than the storm a-blowin'.

(He almost starts to dance, but there is a flash of lightning and BARBARA *clings to him.)*

BARBARA: I'm skeerd! I'm skeerd a lightnin'!

JOHN *(holding her in his arms)*: You ain't got no need a fear. Cause I love you, Barbara Allen. I'm a man, and you a woman, and we got at least a year.

(He kisses her as the lightning flashes, and the stage goes black after it.)

Scene III

The scene is outside the Allen cabin on Chunky Gal Mountain. There is a table, a few chairs. FLOYD ALLEN, *a boy of 15, is playing his guitar and singing.*

FLOYD:

  Down in the valley, the valley so low,
  Hang yer haid low, hear the wind blow.
  Hear the wind blowing, hear the wind blow,
  Hang yer haid low, dear, hear the wind blow.

MRS: ALLEN *(offstage)*: Floyd Allen! You slopped them hawgs yit?

FLOYD: No, Maw. I'm busy.

(He goes on singing.)

  All that I've done, dear, I've done fer yer sake,
  Throw yer arms 'round me, feel my heart break
  Feel my heart breakin', feel my heart break,
  Throw yer arms 'round me, feel my heart break.

(MRS. ALLEN comes in with a pail of milk.)

MRS. ALLEN: You better git to them hawgs, boy, afore hit git dark.

FLOYD: Seem like hawgs git hit mighty easy. Wisht I was a hawg. Be glad when hit hawg-killin' time.

MRS. ALLEN: The signs ain't right yit, son. Got to slop the hawgs till the signs git right.

FLOYD: But hit aready frost, Maw.

MRS. ALLEN: That don't make no never mind. Scorpio ain't outen his eighth house yit, and the zodiac don't lie.

(*She gets out a churn and pours the milk into it.*)

FLOYD: Social worker say the almanac don't know.

MRS. ALLEN: Social worker say a heap aside her prayers. She edicated. Whar yer paw?

FLOYD: He out in the back house.

MRS. ALLEN (*sitting down with the churn before her*): Tell him I wants to see him when he through.

(FLOYD *begins playing and singing.* MRS. ALLEN *joins in with him.*)

FLOYD AND MRS. ALLEN:

>A pure gal left her mother, she were far away from home,
>She walked the streets a Asheville, so cold and so alone.
>A man he come up to her, and he tuck her by the arm,
>And said, "Now I'll be good to you, and see you have no harm."
>He tuck her down a back street, into a house of sin,
>And wunst that pore gal went inside, she never come out agin.
>Jes' a pitcher from life's other side,
>Somebody who fell by the way,
>A life has gone out with the tide, the tide,
>That might of been happy some day, some day.
>Some pore ole mother at home alone,
>Waitin' and watchin' in vain,
>Waitin' to hear, from a loved one so dear—
>Jes' a pitcher from life's other side.

(FLOYD *goes out.*)

MRS. ALLEN: You git them hawgs slopped proper now, boy, afore you through.

(MR. ALLEN *comes on with a shotgun.*)

MR. ALLEN: Seem like jes' can't git nobody to marry Barbara.

MRS. ALLEN: Did you git a chanst to see Marvin Hudgens to-day?

MR. ALLEN: I seed him up at Chunky Gal Gap.

MRS. ALLEN: Didn't you tell him he ought to marry Barbara?

MR. ALLEN: Shore. We argued some, and then he promised me a mule if I'd let him out of it.

MRS. ALLEN: He say he give you he good mule Sally?

MR. ALLEN: Yep. He figgered as how that ought to make things square.

MRS. ALLEN: But he wouldn't marry her.

MR. ALLEN: He figgered as how a mule ought to be worth about as much as a son-in-law.

MRS. ALLEN: Well, what about Rome Agar?

MR. ALLEN: I seed him at the general store in Buck Creek.

MRS. ALLEN: He ain't got no mule.

MR. ALLEN: No, but he give me eight dollar. That a lot of money.

MRS. ALLEN: Jes' seem like hit more trouble than hit worth to try to keep a reputation.

MR. ALLEN: If Barbara'd jes' make an effort to git herself a man.

MRS. ALLEN: How about Harmon Putnam? Did you git a chanst to see him?

MR. ALLEN: He gittin' married to the Bergen gal.

MRS. ALLEN: He ain't married yit.

MR. ALLEN: But he gonna be next Sunday, and her paw's a friend of mine.

MRS. ALLEN: All the more reason for him to hep us out.

MR. ALLEN: Then who'd marry Ella Bergen? She eight month gone aready.

MRS. ALLEN: Hit seem like somethin' allus stand in the way. Yep, hit look like Barbara'll have to bed a bastard. Gawd know

I told her hit were bound to happen. You can't pleasure yerself ferever without gittin' caught.

(FLOYD *comes back on.*)

FLOYD: Preacher Haggler comin' up the trail.

MRS. ALLEN: He ain't got no cause to be a-callin' on us.

MR. ALLEN: He a man a Gawd, Maw. He got his reasons.

FLOYD: I reckon he here fer to see about Barbara. Reckon he wants her to git sanctified.

MRS. ALLEN: She been washed in the blood a the heavenly Lamb.

MR. ALLEN: Seem like that ought to last her a spell.

(PREACHER HAGGLER *appears.*)

HAGGLER: Howdy, Sister Allen.

MRS. ALLEN: Howdy, Preacher Haggler, howdy.

HAGGLER: Howdy, Brother Allen.

MR. ALLEN: Howdy, Preacher Haggler. Draw up a chair and set a spell.

HAGGLER: Don't mind as how I do. (*He sits.*)

MR. ALLEN: How about some corn?

HAGGLER: Well, if you got it right handy.

MR. ALLEN: No trouble at all, no trouble at all. Son, get the preacher a nip of mountain dew. It fresh out'n the still a week come Wednesday. Best corn licker I made this year.

MRS. ALLEN (*as* FLOYD *gets the jug and hands it to* HAGGLER, *who tilts it over his shoulder and takes a swig*): It sure is that. It sure is that.

HAGGLER (*wiping his mouth*): Brother Allen, I always say, there ain't a man in the church—not a man in the church—can make mountain dew as good as you.

MR. ALLEN: Comin' from you, Preacher, that mighty fine praise.

MRS. ALLEN: We couldn't get our last pastor to tetch a drop.

HAGGLER: He a foot-washin' Baptist, Sister Allen. He ain't seed the light in the right way yit.

(*He takes another pull at the jug.*)

MRS. ALLEN: How come you ain't averse to taking a nip, Preacher?

HAGGLER: It in the Bible, Sister. Good book say wine maketh glad the heart.

MR. ALLEN: Preacher Justice kept a quoting the Scriptures too, but he come up with some of them other passages, like, "Look not upon the wine when it is red." He claimed that mean we ain't supposed to make no beverages.

HAGGLER: He was just showing his ignorance. If Jesus turned water into wine, what's wrong in our converting the corn we grow?

MR. ALLEN: How come we ain't figured that out afore, Ma?

MRS. ALLEN: Besides what we makin' ain't red.

HAGGLER: That the truth. Mountain dew is clear—almost white, with jest a tech of green. And the good Lord hisself knows that green is the color of charity.

MR. ALLEN: I reckon you're right about that.

HAGGLER: Brother Allen, how about a little drop for you?

MR. ALLEN: I could be persuaded, Preacher. I could be persuaded.

(*He takes the jug and drinks.*)

MRS. ALLEN: It sure do my heart good to see a man enjoy his corn.

MR. ALLEN: Maw, how about you?

MRS. ALLEN: Well, just a little maybe, being it's so fine.

HAGGLER (*as she drinks*): Take a long one, Sister. It make the talk flow easy.

FLOYD: Maw, can I have some too?

MRS. ALLEN: You too young, boy.

FLOYD: No, I ain't neither, Maw. I been drinking corn licker since I was ten.

HAGGLER: A drop now and then won't hurt the boy, I reckon. It the best thing there be for a-cleansing of the blood.

FLOYD: Can I, Ma?

MRS. ALLEN: Well, I reckon, bein's how the preacher don't make no never mind.

MR. ALLEN: Don't let him git too much now, Maw.

MRS. ALLEN (*seeing* FLOYD *still drinking*): That enough son. You'll burn out your gut.

(MRS. ALLEN *begins to sing.* FLOYD *accompanies her on his guitar, improvising*)

> Some folks like to dip their snuff,
> Some folks like to chew.
> Me, I get the greatest joy
> By drinking mountain dew.

(*The four join in the chorus:*)

> We're a-stillin', always stillin'
> Since the day we first was born,
> Been a-stillin', still a'stillin'
> That Smokey mountain corn.

MR. ALLEN:

> Some folks live on buttermilk
> And some choose water first.
> But if our corn crops ever fail,
> I know I'll die of thirst.
>
> CHORUS

FLOYD:

> Some folks wear long underwear
> Or poke the fire that's low.
> Me, I'll take a swig of corn
> And let them cold winds blow.-
>
> CHORUS

HAGGLER

> Some folks kneel in prayer at home,
> Some git moved in the pew,
> But the loudest call I ever heard
> Came from mountain dew.
>
> CHORUS

MR. ALLEN: How about another little drop, Preacher?
HAGGLER: I reckon as how I better not.

MR. ALLEN: Well, put the licker up, son, back on the shelf.

(FLOYD *replaces the jug.*)

MRS. ALLEN: Kin I git you somethin' to eat? Got some squirrel meat right here ole man shot this mornin'. Right smart luck with his varmint shootin' this year.

HAGGLER: Thank you, Sister Allen. I've had my supper.

MR. ALLEN: We et, too, jes' afore you come.

HAGGLER: Well, I'll tell you what I come fer. I'm a pastor, Sister Allen, and I looks after my flock.

MR. ALLEN: Hit the Gawd's truth, Lawd.

MRS. ALLEN: Thar ain't a better preacher in the whole Smoky Mountains, leastways not on Chunky Gal from Old Baldy to Buck Creek. Wunst you git started on fire and damnation, seem like hell itself jes' rise right outen the ground. Thar ain't a sinner in the valley kin sit and listen to you without gittin' the spirit and confessin' thar shame.

MR. ALLEN: I ain't fergot how you brung Miz Gudger to salvation last revival—how you yelled at her and hollered and pinted with the hand. The spirit done tuck holt so hard she fell right into the floor. Miz Metcalf, she run up to hep her, but you yelled out at her, "The Lord done flang her thar, let her lay!" Hit were then she started talkin' in the unknown tongue. That were shore a great revival.

HAGGLER: Hit were that, Brother Allen, hit were that.

MRS. ALLEN: I tell you, when hit come to savin' sinners thar ain't nobody like you, Preacher.

MR. ALLEN: That's a natural fact o' Gawd——

HAGGLER: Whenever I hear of a sheep a mine that's strayed, I make off to bring hit right back to the Lord.

MRS. ALLEN: You ain't wrong thar, Preacher.

HAGGLER: Well, I couldn't hep but hear about the dance last Saturday. Edna Summey should have shame for the things she said.

MRS. ALLEN: But hit were the truth, Preacher Haggler. She hadn't oughter said hit, but hit were the Gawd's truth.

HAGGLER: I figgered how hit was, sinst everybody talkin'. And hit made me decide to lend a hepin' hand.

MRS. ALLEN: Hit mighty good a you, Preacher.

HAGGLER: Hit my duty and my pleasure. The thing I wants to do is git Barbara married.

FLOYD: You'll have a hard time a-doin' hit, I kin tell you that right now.

MRS. ALLEN: Floyd, this ain't none a yer affair, so git outen the house.

FLOYD: But, Maw, I wants to listen.

MRS. ALLEN: You heerd what I done tole you.

FLOYD: She a sister of mine. 'Sides I know all about her. She gonna bed a bastard.

MR. ALLEN: This here talk private, so do what yer maw says.

FLOYD (as he leaves): Be glad when I git old. Allus gittin' put out when thar's fun startin'.

HAGGLER: Hit jes' as well you tole the boy to git outen the house, cause what I got to tell you ain't got no truck with young uns.

MR. ALLEN: What is hit, Preacher Haggler?

MRS. ALLEN: Yes, what is hit you want?

HAGGLER: Whar Barbara now, Miz Allen?

MRS. ALLEN: She out thar sommers. I couldn't tell you whar.

HAGGLER: You let her out right often, alone in the night?

MRS. ALLEN: She a growed gal, Preacher. I ain't fer to stop her.

HAGGLER: But you got to take the disgrace when she git herself in trouble.

MRS. ALLEN: I know that, Preacher Haggler, but what kin we do?

HAGGLER: Well, I thought a somethin' fer you. A way to git her married.

MR. ALLEN: That what we're a-wantin'.

MRS. ALLEN: Shore. Tell us what hit be.

HAGGLER: Thar's a feller who's been hangin' 'round, don't nobody know him.

MRS. ALLEN: You mean the stranger who danced with Barbara the other night?

HAGGLER: That him. Well, I seed him agin this afternoon up by Hawg Back Holler. He ain't been here very long, and that's the man you want.

MR. ALLEN: Whar he from?

HAGGLER: Well, now I don't know. I ast him right enough, but he say he come from over on Old Baldy Mounting.

MRS. ALLEN: Why, thar ain't nobody live up thar.

HAGGLER: I know hit, and I told him. But hit don't differ, Sister Allen, if he ain't from these parts here.

MR. ALLEN: I ain't got no truck with furriners.

HAGGLER: But he better'n nobody.

MRS. ALLEN: That right, Preacher.

HAGGLER: Asides, he ain't had a chanst yit to find out about things.

MRS. ALLEN: And you think he marry Barbara?

HAGGLER: Shore, he marry Barbara. He tole me so hisself. He ast me all about her.

MRS. ALLEN: You didn't tell him nothin'?

HAGGLER: Well, I had to tell him somethin'. Hit plain to might nigh everybody what Barbara went and done. So I said hit weren't no fault a hern, that she was to git married, was all ready fer the weddin', when her man he up and died.

MRS. ALLEN: And he believe you?

HAGGLER: Shore he did. Weren't no reason why he shouldn't. Asides I think he still take her if I'd tole him the whole truth.

MRS. ALLEN: Hit'd shore save us a heap a trouble if we could git the gal a husband, and if you say this man want her——

HAGGLER: He want her.

MRS. ALLEN: Why, that good enough fer me.

MR. ALLEN: Well, hit ain't fer me. You don't know nothin' 'bout him.

MRS. ALLEN: He a right smart-lookin' feller, and the way he whopped Marvin Hudgens were a sight to see.

MR. ALLEN: Aw, he whop him too easy. He didn't never tetch him. I was a-standin' right thar and I seed the whole fight.

HAGGLER: Well, you'll git a chanst to see him soon and you kin ast him how he done hit. He say he comin' over to see you to-night.

MRS. ALLEN: You reckon he means hit, what he say about Barbara?

HAGGLER: I don't see why he got a cause fer to tell you a lie.

MR. ALLEN: Hit jes' seem quare somehow.

HAGGLER: Well, you all will figger hit out some way. And now I reckon I better be gittin' on home.

(*He gets up.*)

MR. ALLEN: Don't go yit, Preacher Haggler. Set with us a week.

HAGGLER: Cain't, I reckon. Come go over the mounting with me.

MR. ALLEN: Can't, I reckon. You stay with us.

HAGGLER: Can't, I reckon.

(*He goes out.*)

MRS. ALLEN: Preacher Haggler a mighty fine man.

MR. ALLEN: Shore a fine feller.

FLOYD (*running on*): Paw, Paw. Thar an eagle out thar, Paw. Hit a-flyin' low and callin'. I reckon hit the biggest eagle I ever see.

MRS. ALLEN: Hit after the chickens. Did you shet the henhouse?

FLOYD: Shore I shet it, Maw. He can't do us no harm. But hit shore is a big un.

MR. ALLEN: Hand me down my hawg rifle, son. I'll see if I kin git him.

FLOYD: Let me try hit, Paw. I'm shore I kin git him.

MR. ALLEN: I said *I'd* git him, and I don't mean you.

(*He takes the gun which* FLOYD *has picked up.* JOHN *has suddenly appeared.*)

JOHN: I'm lookin' fer Barbara Allen.

MRS. ALLEN: She ain't here right now.

JOHN: This here her house, ain't hit?

MRS. ALLEN: I reckon. Won't you come in and set a spell.

JOHN: I reckon.

MR. ALLEN: Draw you up a char thar by the fire. Barbara be comin' in purty soon.

FLOYD: Paw, let me shoot the eagle. Please give me the gun.

JOHN: Ain't no eagle out thar.

FLOYD: But I seed him, Mister.

JOHN: Thar ain't no eagle out thar. Go back and look.

FLOYD: Kin I take the gun, Paw?

MR. ALLEN: I reckon you kin have her.

(FLOYD *takes the gun and runs off.* JOHN *watches, a little anxiously.* MR. ALLEN *calls after* FLOYD.)

But don't go wastin' shot lest you sight her fair and true.

MRS. ALLEN (*to* JOHN): Kin I git you some supper?

JOHN: Well, I am right hungry.

MRS. ALLEN: Hit won't take fer long.

(BARBARA *appears, looking after* FLOYD. *She sees* JOHN *and comes on.*)

MR. ALLEN: Whar you been, Barbara?

BARBARA (*to* JOHN, *as he turns and sees her*): What you doin' here?

JOHN: I come here to ast yer maw and paw a question. I want to ast thar leave to make you my wife.

MR. ALLEN: But we don't hardly know you, yer name or whar you come from.

JOHN: Hit don't differ whar I come from, cause hit here I'm gonna stay.

MR. ALLEN: But yer maw and yer paw——

MRS. ALLEN: Hit don't make no difference. If Barbara a mind to hit, I reckon hit all right.

MR. ALLEN: But, Maw——

MRS. ALLEN: If Preacher Haggler say hit the Lord's will——

MR. ALLEN: But seem like we ought to tell him what Barbara went and done.

JOHN: I aready know that, Mr. Allen. Preacher Haggler done tole me. But hit don't make no never mind if Barbara be my wife.

MRS. ALLEN: What you say, gal? Will you have him?

BARBARA: You'll be takin' quite a chanst if you marry me.

MR. ALLEN: No more chanst than you be takin', gal, is what I'm thinkin'.

BARBARA: What the matter, Paw? Don't you want fer me to marry?

MR. ALLEN: I reckon, since hit seem like the only chanst you'll git.

BARBARA: Why, thar's lots a fellers, Paw, that's wantin' me to marry.

MR. ALLEN: Shore. They want you to marry someone else.

MRS. ALLEN: Hesh your mouth! You ain't got no right to be a-talkin' that-a-way about yer own daughter.

JOHN: Will you, Barbara Allen? I'm a-waitin' fer yer answer.

BARBARA: My answer is yes, cause I couldn't tell you no.

MRS. ALLEN: Well now that right fine. I know you both be happy.

(*There is the sound of a shot offstage.*)

MR. ALLEN: Did you git him, Floyd boy? Did you git the eagle?

FLOYD (*offstage*): Naw, he git away, Paw.

JOHN: Tole you that weren't no eagle out thar.

MR. ALLEN: But Floyd said he seed hit.

MRS. ALLEN: Well, perhaps he were wrong. I reckon you two got things you want to talk about.

BARBARA: I reckon, Maw.

MRS. ALLEN: Well, we be a-goin'. Hit gittin' late nohow.

MR. ALLEN: I ain't a-goin' till hit time fer bed.

MRS. ALLEN: With yer daughter gittin' married, you'll do like I say. Now git on up thar and leave 'em be.

(*She pushes* ALLEN *ahead of her up the stairs and out.*)

JOHN (*gazing at* BARBARA): Barbara!

BARBARA: Yes?

JOHN: I don't care what the Conjur Woman say, you the purtiest gal in all the world.

BARBARA: The Conjur Woman? You been talkin' to her?

JOHN: I reckon.

BARBARA: What you messin' 'round with her fer?

JOHN: I—I had to ast her to do somethin' fer me.

BARBARA: Thar ain't nothin' she can do fer you, nothin' that ain't bad. You got stay clear a them conjur folks if you and me is married. The blood a the Jesus Lamb give us all the power we need.

JOHN: No Jesus lamb blood gonna hep me out.

BARBARA: Ain't you a Christian?

JOHN: I reckon not.

BARBARA: I ain't never knowed no one who weren't a Christian afore.

JOHN: You mean you won't marry me lest I'm washed in the blood?

BARBARA: I didn't say that, did I? Thar time enough later fer you to git salvation. Jes' so you love me, that all I ast.

JOHN: I love you, Barbara Allen. I promise you that.

(*He takes her in his arms and kisses her.* DARK WITCH *appears from a tree.*)

DARK WITCH: Witch boy! What you doin' in thar? What you doin' in a house a humans?

JOHN: I reckon I got my reasons.

(THE FAIR WITCH *appears over the edge of the roof.*)

FAIR WITCH: Why you want to be a human? Don't you know you'll be sorry?

DARK WITCH: Conjur Woman jes' change you to plague you with a trick.

FAIR WITCH: And yer eagle gittin' lonesome. You can't ride the sky without him.

DARK WITCH: And I git lonesome, witch boy. I git lonesome too.

JOHN: Tain't no affair a mine.

DARK WITCH: She ain't purty! Hit jes' you that thinks so.

FAIR WITCH: Would you leave us, witch boy? Leave us fer a human?

(*Both* WITCHES *disappear.*)

JOHN: I done made up my mind, and thar ain't no turning back.

BARBARA (*moving away from him enough to look at him*): What the matter, John boy? You look like you been seein' witches in the night?

JOHN: I was thinkin' a some friends—some friends I used to know. They're fur away now.

BARBARA: I love you, John boy. You kin kiss me if you like.

(JOHN *starts to kiss her, but is interrupted by* MARVIN HUD-GENS, *who comes on.* JOHN *hides in the shadows.*)

MARVIN: Good evenin', Barbara Allen. Kin I talk to you a minute?

BARBARA: I reckon.

MARVIN (*coming on slowly*): I been thinkin' over what yer paw say to-day, and I figgered as how I made up my mind too quick.

BARBARA: What Paw been a-tellin' you?

MARVIN: He 'lowed as how you and me ought to git married. Now I ain't never been averse to the ideer, but I like to do my own courtin' in my own way and in my own time.

BARBARA: Well, hit ain't none a Paw's affair.

MARVIN: That's how I figgered. A feller don't like to be pushed into nothin' like that, so I kinda balked at his tellin' me what to do. I even promised him my ole mule Sally if he'd fergit about hit. But sinst then I been a-thinkin' things out. I figgered as how I need old Sally right smart, so I come here to ast you to be my wife.

JOHN (*suddenly coming forward*): I'm afraid you jes' a little too late, Marvin Hudgens. Will you be a-goin' now, or do you want *I* should count three?

MARVIN: I—I'll be a-goin' now, if that's how things is standin'.

JOHN: That's how things is standin'.

(MARVIN *goes sullenly off, and* BARBARA *goes to* JOHN *and takes his hand.*)

BARBARA: You shore manage him proper, John. I'm mighty proud to marry you.

(JOHN *leads her off and they walk, his arm around her, into the night. The sound of an eagle call is heard.* JOHN *hesitates and is looking back towards the eagle cry as the lights dim.*)

Scene IV

The general store of Buck Creek, shelves, counter, stove, chairs, and a large apple barrel. MR. SUMMEY, *the owner, is behind the counter.* ATKINS *and* BERGEN *are playing checkers, and* BURT DINWITTY *is taking an apple from the barrel.* SMELICUE *is playing his guitar and singing.* FLOYD ALLEN *is listening.*

SMELICUE:
  John Williams, John Williams, please tell me yer mind,
  Is yer mind fer to marry me, or leave me behind?
  He jump on he pony, and away he did ride,
  And he tuck Little Onie along by he side.
OTHERS:
  And he tuck Little Onie along by he side.
SMELICUE:
  They come to a river, a river so wide,
  John Williams dismounted with the gal by he side,
  John Williams, John Williams, please tell me yer mind,
  Is yer mind fer to marry me or leave me behind?
OTHERS:
  Is yer mind fer to marry me or leave me behind?

(HANK GUDGER *comes in and also steals an apple.*)

SMELICUE:
  He hugged her, he kissed her, he turned her around.
  And he throwed her in the water whare he knowed she would
    drowned.

OTHERS:
　　And he throwed her in the water whar he knowed she would
　　drowned.

HANK: You fellers a-settin' around and a-singin' shore prove hit
　　gittin' colder weather.

ATKINS: Yep. Hit hawg-killin' time fer shore now. Gormans
　　was a-killin' a sow this mornin'. Finest chanst a hawg meat
　　as ever I seed.

MR. BERGEN: Frost come early this year.

SMELICUE: Hit a bad sign, a bad sign. Frost in September, a
　　death afore November.

HANK: Aw, folks is a-dyin' most any time. (*He laughs.*)

SMELICUE: Hit ain't no laughin' matter, son. You hear what I'm
　　a-sayin. Things is a-happenin' that ain't the will a Gawd.

MR. BERGEN: Why, ain't nothin' happenin' without Gawd first
　　a-willin'. All He gotta do is make up He mind.

SMELICUE: But thar still some several that got the jump on
　　Jesus. They got the powers a darkness, headin' straight from
　　hell.

ATKINS: You ain't wrong thar, Uncle Smelicue.

SMELICUE: I know what I'm a-sayin'.

BURT: You right, Uncle Smelicue. They got the powers a darkness
　　headin' straight from hell.

SMELICUE: Why, Mr. Riddle was a-tellin' me jes' last nite how
　　he wife wanted back the ring thar daughter Agnes wore.

ATKINS: The ring with the green stone that shined in the
　　darkness?

MR. BERGEN: The ring Jed Higgins give her afore he cut her
　　throat?

MR. SUMMEY: The ring that got caught and they couldn't git
　　hit off her, so they left hit on the finger a her cold dead hand?

SMELICUE: Well, Mr. Riddle was a-sayin' as how he wife figgered
　　that by now the hand ought to be shrunk enough to pry hit
　　loose.

MR. SUMMEY: But Agnes Riddle buried.

MR. BERGEN: She grounded in the graveyard.

BURT: Grounded in the graveyard, under six feet a dirt.

ATKINS, MR. BERGEN AND HANK: Under six feet a dirt.

MR. SUMMEY AND BURT: Under six feet a dirt.

SMELICUE: Well, I reckon they knowed hit, but hit didn't differ, so they git them a lantern and a shovel and a spade.

OTHERS: And a shovel and a spade, and a shovel and a spade.

SMELICUE: And they starts a-diggin', in the night time they a-diggin', diggin' in the blackness with jes' a lantern fer a light.

ATKINS: And they git to the coffin?

MR. BERGEN: And they git the coffin open?

HANK: And they git at the ring with the green and shinin' stone.

SMELICUE: Well, they git to the coffin, and they git the coffin open, but the ring hit gone, and the hand chopped off!

OTHERS: And the hand chopped off!

SMELICUE: And the face all black and swollen, and the eyes wide and starin', and the hair most all pulled out by the roots.

HANK: Who coulda done hit?

SMELICUE: Twarn't nobody human.

BURT: You mean hit were a witch?

SMELICUE: Ain't no doubt about hit. Hit were a witch, as shore as the Lord.

ALL: Hit were a witch, all right, hit were a witch!

BURT: I'm skeered!

MR. SUMMEY: Why, thar ain't nothin' to be skeered about. Ain't you been saved by the grace a the Lord Jesus Christ?

BURT: Yeah, but witches they is different. They kin conjur folks, and a-chase 'em and a-hound 'em and a ride 'em till they're dead.

MR. SUMMEY: Then you best be mindin' what I tell you. Jes' don't give 'em no chanst to git a holt on you. (MISS METCALF comes in.) Howdy, Miss Metcalf.

MISS METCALF: Howdy.

SMELICUE: Howdy, Miss Metcalf. How's things with you?

MISS METCALF: Jes' gittin' along past common, I reckon. (*She turns to* SUMMEY.) Oh, Mr. Summey. I'd like to look at some calico. Thought I'd use the weddin' fer an excuse to make me a new dress.

MR. SUMMEY: Ella Bergen and Harmon Putnam gittin' married tomorrer. You'll have to work real fast to git hit made in time.

MISS METCALF: Hit ain't that weddin' I'm a-talkin' about.

MR. BERGEN: Why, who else is gittin' married?

MISS METCALF: Ain't you heerd the news yit? Barbara Allen's the bride.

FLOYD: Yep, Barbara finally gittin' married.

ATKIN: So Marvin Hudgens gonna do the right thing.

MISS METCALF: Can't say he's a-aimin' to do the right thing a-tall. Hit that new feller from over Baldy way.

MR. BERGEN: The one that rassled Marvin?

MISS METCALF: That him. He a right powerful lookin' feller.

BURT: He didn't rassle fair—he didn't hardly tetch him.

HANK: When's to be the weddin'?

MISS METCALF: I don't know for shore yit.

FLOYD: Jes' as soon's they kin, Maw says.

HANK: So Barbara gittin' married.

SMELICUE: No reason why she oughtn't. She a sight purtier'n a June bug in a tin dipper.

MISS METCALF (*examining cloth* SUMMEY *has unrolled from a bolt*): She purty, maybe.

MR. SUMMEY: She ain't not purtier'n you, Miss Metcalf.

MISS METCALF: Well, she a lot younger. (*She and* SUMMEY *handle several bolts of calico during the following.*)

MR. BERGEN: Age ain't got nothin' to do with hit. Miss Greeny Gorman was all a fifty, and hit didn't holt her back none.

BURT: Yeah, but look who she married to.

SMELICUE: How come you ain't never married, Miss Metcalf? A fetchin' woman like you! (MISS METCALF *giggles.*) But I s'pose a man's hard to git.

MISS METCALF: You right thar, Uncle Smelicue. Hit hard shore enough, and that a fact a Gawd.

(SMELICUE *strums a chord and begins singing, with the others joining in.*)

SMELICUE:

Oh, hit's hard and hit's hard, ain't hit hard,
To love one who never did love you,
And hit's hard, and hit's hard, ain't hit hard, great Gawd,
To love one who never could be true.

(*He sings alone.*)

Now who will kiss her ruby lips?

HANK:

And who will hold her to his breast?

FLOYD:

And who will be her own true lover?

MISS METCALF:

I want some one to love me best.

ALL:

But hit's hard and hit's hard, ain't hit hard,
To love one who never did love you,
And hit's hard and hit's hard, ain't hit hard, great Gawd.

(MISS METCALF *suddenly remembers her dignity.*)

MISS METCALF: Silly men! (*She turns back to the calico as they sing the last line.*)

OTHERS:

To love one who never could be true.

(PREACHER HAGGLER *enters as they finish singing.*)

HAGGLER: The Lord be with you, brothers.

THE MEN: Howdy, Preacher Haggler.

HAGGLER: Howdy, Miss Metcalf.

MISS METCALF: Howdy.

HAGGLER: You're lookin' mighty peert, Brother Smelicue.

SMELICUE: I'm as peert as a cut-tail lizard.

HAGGLER (*seeing* FLOYD): Floyd Allen, yer maw's been lookin' all over fer you. She wants you to git the chores done afore supper.

FLOYD: Now that Barbara gittin' married I gotta do all the work.

(*He gets up and goes out.*)

MR. BERGEN: You go on home, Floyd.

MISS METCALF: Oh, Preacher Haggler, I'd like yore opinion. Which a these calicos'd look purtiest on me.

HAGGLER: That hard to say, hit hard to say. Hit like gildin' the lily.

MISS METCALF: Oh, Preacher Haggler!

HAGGLER: You always dress real fancy.

SMELICUE: That what I been a-tellin' her, Preacher.

HAGGLER: Like the good book say, Solomon in all he glory was not arrayed like one a these.

MISS METCALF (*with a coy laugh*): Well, I jes' can't decide atween this red one and the blue flowers.

HAGGLER: The blue flowers is real purty.

MISS METCALF: Yes, ain't hit now? (*To* SUMMEY.) How much is hit?

MR. SUMMEY: Fifteen cent a yard.

MISS METCALF: I'll take six yard. (*To* HAGGLER.) The other a little tacky. (*She touches the blue again.*) Hit a stout piece a calico.

HAGGLER: Yes—it is.

SMELICUE: That sound a mite skimpy to me, Miss Metcalf. You shore you kin git a good swingy skirt outen only six yard?

MISS METCALF: I kin git a swing outa most anythin' if I git a chanst, Uncle Smelicue. (*She goes back to* SUMMEY, *who is measuring the cloth, and they finish the transaction during the following.*)

(MARVIN HUDGENS *strolls in and watches the checker game.*)

HANK: Howdy, Marvin Hudgens. You heerd about the weddin'?

MARVIN: Yeah, I heerd about the weddin'. What hit to you?

HANK: Why, nothin'. Nothin' a-tall, I reckon. Jes' seem like someone else is a-carryin' off yore gal.

MARVIN: I don't like the way you talkin'. I coulda had her if I wanted.

SMELICUE: Seem like I heerd her pappy say durn nigh the same thing.

MARVIN: Anyway, I coulda married her, and don't you fergit hit. (*He shakes a finger menacingly at* SMELICUE.)

SMELICUE: Take care, take care, take care!

MARVIN: Asides, I play fair. I don't have to spell folks to git what I want.

HAGGLER: What you mean, spell?

MARVIN: I ain't a-sayin'. All I know is what I knows.

MR. BERGEN: He still mad about the rasslin'.

ATKINS: But he were beaten fair and square.

MARVIN: I don't call what he done fair and square. He struck at me with the lightnin'.

SMELICUE: Heah. Lightnin' in both fists.

MARVIN: Hit were real lightnin' that knocked me over. (JOHN *and* BARBARA *come in and hear the next line.*) But I could beat him if I tried again.

JOHN: You kin try hit, if you wanta. Any time, I'll be a-waitin'.

BARBARA: Hit a right stout man I'm a-marryin'. I reckon he the strongest man in all the valley.

MARVIN: He ain't as strong as I am—when hit come to liftin' weights.

JOHN: Lemme see you, Marvin Hudgens. Lemme see you do some liftin'.

MARVIN: I kin lift that barrel thar plumb offen the floor. I kin lift hit up and hold hit high, and not spill nary a apple.

BURT: Shore you kin, Marvin. Show him how you do hit.

MR. SUMMEY: Hit a mighty heavy barrel.

ATKINS: And hit plumb full a apples.

MARVIN: Hit don't differ, not with me. You jes' give me room and watch.

(*The crowd falls back and* MARVIN *goes over to the barrel amid an eager chorus of encouragement and speculation.* BARBARA *and* JOHN *simply watch.* MARVIN *grasps the barrel in his arms and with a good deal of grunting finally lifts it and carries it five or six feet, then sets it down wearily. The* GROUP *gathers round to shake his hand.*)

HANK: Miss Metcalf, come up and shake hands with a mighty stout man.

ATKINS: I knowed he could do hit.

BURT: Strongest man in this here county.

MARVIN (*turning triumphantly to* JOHN): Well, stranger, you kin try hit if you wants.

JOHN: I reckon as how I wants to. You jes' give me room and watch.

SMELICUE: Care to make a little bet, Preacher?

HAGGLER: Hit agin the Gospel, Brother Smelicue. I never gamble.

(*Again the* GROUP *speculates as* JOHN *goes over to the barrel. He gets set and grasps the barrel's top rim with his left hand. As he lifts his left arm the barrel rises until it is shoulder height, then slowly settles back to the floor.*)

MISS METCALF: Look! Hit the doin's a the devil.

HAGGLER: Ain't that somethin' else!

MARVIN: What I tell you 'bout spell? (*He runs out the door.*)

BURT (*following* MARVIN): Hit spelled fer shore!

HANK: He got the powers a darkness.

SMELICUE: Who'd a thunk hit!

(JOHN *turns back to* BARBARA *and* HAGGLER.)

BARBARA: Hit a real man I'm a-marryin'.

HAGGLER: I ain't never seen no man who could do nothin' like that!

BARBARA: Well, the longer you live the more you larn.

HAGGLER: And when were you plannin' on gittin' married?

JOHN: Hit about that we come to see you, Preacher. We figgered the sooner we married the better.

HAGGLER: Thar aready one weddin' in the church tomorrer. How about yourn a week from then?

JOHN: I don't reckon as how we kin wait that long.

SMELICUE: Claims they can't wait, hey, Miss Metcalf?

MISS METCALF: Look to me like they ain't waited a-tall.

JOHN: What that you a-sayin'?

MISS METCALF: What I means is, thar ain't no sense in waitin' when yer mind's made up.

SMELICUE: Mind's made up fer what, Miss Metcalf?

MISS METCALF: To have the weddin' is what I means.

SMELICUE: Oh!

JOHN: That's what we done figgered, so, Preacher, we'd like to git married right away.

HAGGLER: Have you told yer folks about hit?

BARBARA: Why, they is willin'. They be right glad to git me married any time.

SMELICUE: That' right. Her paw looked kinda questionin' like at me wunst.

HAGGLER: You means you wants to git married to-day?

JOHN: That the ideer exactly. We wants to git married to-day and right now.

MISS METCALF: They shore in a hurry.

JOHN: Can't you do hit?

HAGGLER: I reckon hit might could be arranged. You got to git a permit.

JOHN: Can't you git hit fer us?

HAGGLER: Got one right here. Two dollar and a half.

(*He takes a folded paper out of his pocket.*)

JOHN: I ain't got no two dollar and a half. That one thing I didn't figger.

BARBARA: I got the money, John, right here in my pocket. (*She takes some bills and change out.*) Here one, two, two dollar and fifty cent.

HANK: That only fifty cent more'n the price a sin.

SMELICUE: Sinnin' shore gone sky-high sinst my time.

HAGGLER (*pocketing the money* BARBARA *counted out*): This ain't no time to be speakin' a the flesh. This here's legal. (*He turns to* JOHN *and offers him the paper and a pencil.*) Now all you gotta do is fill in the spaces.

JOHN: I'm sorry, Preacher Haggler, but I can't read or write.

HAGGLER: I reckon I kin do hit fer you. The first question is, what's yer name?

JOHN: My name John.

HAGGLER (*writing*): John what?

JOHN: Jes' John.

MISS METCALF: You ain't a bastard, are you?

JOHN: Well, not exactly.

HAGGLER: You got to have a last name.

MISS METCALF: Ain't he got no last name?

HAGGLER: You got have a last name to put on the blank.

JOHN: You kin put down—Human! That my name, John Human.

HAGGLER (*writing it*): Human. I ain't never heerd that name afore. How old are you?

JOHN: I don't rightly know.

HAGGLER: I'll say twenty-three. You got to put down somethin'.

JOHN: I'm twenty-three, then. But if things work out, I'll git eternal life.

HAGGLER: Amen, brother. That a fine way fer a Christian to talk. . . . You been baptized, ain't you?

JOHN: Nope, I ain't never been baptized.

OTHERS: Ain't never been baptized?

HAGGLER: Have you been sprinkled?

JOHN: Not as how I remember.

HAGGLER: I pray to Gawd fer the Holy Ghost to move you. We be havin' a revival in another month.

MR. SUMMEY: Amen, Preacher Haggler. Holy Ghost'll git him when you start preachin' hellfire, sin and damnation.

SMELICUE: He be right thar on the mourners' bench, shoutin' halleluiah and a-callin' to he Gawd.

ALL: Amen, praise be holy name, halleluiah, etc.

BARBARA (*as* JOHN *starts to protest*): One thing at a time. Let's git on with the weddin'. My name Barbara Allen and I'm nineteen year next month.

SMELICUE: She shore done a heap a livin' in nineteen year.

HAGGLER: Well, if you shore you wants the weddin' to-day, let's go gettin' on over to the church.

JOHN: This here ain't no church weddin', preacher.

HAGGLER: Whar else do you want hit?

JOHN: We wants to git married right here.

HAGGLER: I ain't never heerd a no weddin' in no general store. Hit ain't Christian nor proper.

JOHN: I ain't ast fer no Christian weddin'.

MISS METCALF: Why, that sin and damnation. . . . You got to git married in the eyes a the Lord.

JOHN: I don't care who a-lookin', but I ain't gittin' married in no church a Gawd.

OTHERS: He ain't gittin' married in no church a Gawd.

JOHN: I wants to git married, so git started, Preacher.

BARBARA: You better do like he say. He a mighty stout man.

HAGGLER: I reckon I kin do hit. Good Book say, wherever you are gathered together in my name thar will I be also. Let us pray. O my Jesus, look down on this here man and this woman.

OTHERS: Amen, Lord.

HAGGLER: Show 'em the way a Gawd and a light. Make 'em turn from the paths a wickedness and derision. Cleanse 'em by the light a yer Grace.

OTHERS: Amen, Jesus.

(*During the prayer,* BARBARA *stands with bowed head.* JOHN *looks at her in surprise, and in growing fury at the others, who are getting the spirit of salvation.*)

HAGGLER: Show 'em, Gawd, the fruit a thar sin, wash 'em in the blood a the lamb.

OTHERS: Wash 'em in the blood a the lamb.

JOHN (*exploding*): If this here a weddin', let's git the prayin' done with. We wants to git married, and git married fast.

HAGGLER: We ain't never so rushed we can't take time to talk with the Lord.

JOHN: I ain't meanin' to interrupt no important conversations, but we in a hurry to git married.

BARBARA: That right, Preacher Haggler. You better do like John say. He a powerful man, and he ain't amin' to be crossed.

HAGGLER: Well, jine yer right hands. (*They do so.*) Dearly beloved, we are gathered together in the sight a Gawd and this company to jine this here man and this woman in the holy bonds of matrimony. Good Book say that a man shall leave his father and his mother and shall cleave to his wife. John, do you take this woman to be yer lawful wedded wife, in sickness or in health, fer richer or fer poorer, fer better or fer worse, to love, honor and cherish, till death do you part?

JOHN: Till death do us part!

HAGGLER: Answer, I do.

JOHN: I do.

HAGGLER: Barbara, do you take this man to be yer lawful wedded husband, in sickness or in health, fer richer or fer poorer, fer better or fer worse, to love, honor and obey, till death do you part?

BARBARA: I do.

HAGGLER: Afore Gawd and this company, what token do you give to signify this act?

JOHN: Token?

HAGGLER: Ain't you got a ring?

JOHN: I ain't got no ring.

ALL: Ain't he got a ring?

SMELICUE: You can't have a weddin' without no ring.

JOHN (*suddenly*): I got a ring! (*He pulls a ring from a string around his neck.*) Here the ring.

HAGGLER: Place hit on her finger and repeat after me. With this ring I do thee wed.

JOHN (*putting the ring on* BARBARA's *finger*): With this ring I do thee wed.

HAGGLER: Whom Gawd hath jined together let no man put asunder. And now, kiss the bride.

(BARBARA *and* JOHN *kiss.* SMELICUE *comes up to kiss her, but* HAGGLER *waves him back.* BARBARA *looks admiringly at her hand.*)

BARBARA: Hit shore a purty ring. John. Hit shore a purty ring.

JOHN: Hit got a green stone, Barbara. A green stone that shine in the dark!

(*He kisses her again, as the crowd looks at* BARBARA'S *hand with horror.*)

ALL: That shine in the dark!

CURTAIN

ACT TWO

Scene I

The scene is a clearing in the woods near JOHN'S *and* BARBARA'S *cabin.* JOHN *has been chopping wood. He is hacking away awkwardly at a large log, and it is evident that this work is something which he is not used to. After several clumsy strokes, he sets the axe down and wipes his forehead. He stands a moment, angry with himself, but his attention is soon diverted by the sounds of the wood. He stretches, then begins to dance, but recalls himself and lies down along the log. Behind him the* FAIR WITCH *appears. She dances over to him and gets his attention, and he begins to dance with her. The* DARK WITCH *comes in, and he joins them in a gay free dance which recalls the life he left to become human. Suddenly* BARBARA *is heard calling offstage.*

BARBARA (*offstage*): John!

(*He stops dancing, and turns towards the sound, but the witches surround him and stop him.*)

Whar are you, John!

(*Again he starts toward her, but the witches pull him back with them.*)

John!

(*He jumps away from the witches and motions them to leave, which they do slowly.*)

Whar are you, John!

(*He relaxes, then looks around to be sure they are gone.*)

JOHN: I'm over here, Barbara. I'm over here.

BARBARA (*entering and looking at the log*): You didn't git much wood chopped, did you?

JOHN: I reckon not. But I guess hit enough to last till spring.

BARBARA (*setting down the basket she is carrying*): Last till spring! Lord Gawd, boy! You gone outa yer senses? That ain't hardly enough to last us one day.

44

JOHN: I reckon hit take more'n I figgered.

BARBARA (*sitting beside him*): I reckon hit do. Git real cold in the mounting in the winter. Take a heap o' wood to see us through.

JOHN: I git to hit agin after awhile. Gotta rest sometime.

BARBARA (*indicating the basket*): I brought you some lunch. Cawn bread and hawg back.

JOHN: Thank you, Barbara. Reckon's how I couldn't git on without you.

BARBARA: That ain't nothin'. Wife allus gits vittles fer her husband.

JOHN: But ain't all the wives as purty as you. You the purtiest gal in the whole valley. (*He kisses her.*)

BARBARA: And you the finest man. And hit don't differ what the others say.

JOHN: What others? What they sayin', Barbara?

BARBARA: Hit jes' cause they jealous. That what make 'em say things.

JOHN: What things?

BARBARA: Hit don't differ, really hit don't. I don't pay 'em no never mind.

JOHN: But who talkin', Barbara? Who sayin' things?

BARBARA: Folks in church last Sunday. They was talkin' 'bout you.

JOHN: What they say?

BARBARA: They say thar somethin' wrong, that you ain't like no other person.

JOHN: Everybody different, I reckon.

BARBARA: But they sayin' you more different than most. 'Course that true and I ain't complainin', but several say somethin' real bad agin you.

JOHN: What real bad thing do they say?

BARBARA: You won't git mad if I tell you?

JOHN: I won't git mad.

BARBARA: They 'lowed you a witch.

JOHN: Who say that?

BARBARA: Uncle Smelicue, and Miss Metcalf, and thar were some others.

JOHN: They liars! I ain't no witch!

BARBARA: I know hit, John boy. I tell 'em. But hit bad fer 'em to think so.

JOHN: Hit don't differ what they think.

BARBARA: But I don't want 'em to think things that ain't true.

JOHN: I'm a man like anybody. Conjur Woman tole me so.

BARBARA: Then why not prove hit to 'em. Hit so easy if you wants. Hit so easy if you willin'.

JOHN: I tole you wunst, and I'll say hit again. I can't never set foot in no house a Gawd.

BARBARA: But if you jes' do hit wunst, John. Jes' do hit wunst and git fire from the Lord. Git washed in the blood and saved by the grace, and then they know fer shore you ain't no witch.

JOHN: I can't do hit, Barbara. That one thing I can't never do.

BARBARA: Not even fer me? Not even if I ast hit?

JOHN: No, Barbara, not even fer you.

BARBARA: I'll never ast you agin, John.

JOHN: But you believe me, don't you? You believe me when I say I ain't no witch?

BARBARA: I reckon. Hit don't differ what nobody else say. What nobody else think. I believe you, John. I believe what you tell me.

JOHN: I'm a-tellin' you the truth. I ain't no witch.

(MARVIN *strolls in.*)

MARVIN: Howdy, Barbara. Howdy, John.

JOHN: Howdy, Marvin Hudgens.

MARVIN (*looking at the log*): Gittin' yer wood cut fer winter?

JOHN: I reckon.

MARVIN: Ain't much good at choppin', are you?

JOHN: I kin do all right without yore help.

MARVIN: Seem like you need the hep a someone. That ain't hardly fittin' wood to burn.

BARBARA: John ain't had much practice choppin'. He larn how when he has more time.

MARVIN: Choppin' ain't no conjur magic. I reckon you done found that out. Ain't like raisin' apple barrels, ain't like winnin' a rasslin' match.

JOHN: I kin chop as good as anybody.

MARVIN: You call what you been doin' choppin'? Yer log ain't split half even, and the branches still on. Here, lemme show you, boy. Lemme show you some real choppin'.

(*He goes over to the log and picks up the axe. His strokes are long and even and accent his words.*)

You got to *hit* that log with *all* yer strength,
Long broad strokes of even length,
Jes' one way to chop *wood,* 'low,
*Mar*vin Hudgens *show* you how!

(*He sets the axe down and comes back to* BARBARA *and* JOHN.)
Hit all in knowin' how to do hit, boy. Hit all in knowin' how.

JOHN: I reckon you think you right smart.

MARVIN: I reckon. When you larn to chop like that I'll show you some more. Pore Barbara Allen. I'm right sorry fer you.

JOHN: Ain't no need to be.

MARVIN: I reckon she did the best she could fer herself.

BARBARA: I'm satisfied, Marvin Hudgens, and I ain't astin' no hep from you.

MARVIN: Seems to me you'll need the hep a someone I'm a-thinkin'. How soon yer confinement come?

BARBARA: Most any day now, Miz Summey say.

MARVIN: Then what you do, John boy? What you do when she take to her bed?

JOHN: I reckon I make out.

MARVIN: And who cook fer you and do all the work while you loafin' in the field or a layin' in the hay?

BARBARA: Don't fret yerself about us, Marvin Hudgens. We ain't complainin'. We git along.

JOHN: That right, Marvin. We git along.

BARBARA: I better be gittin' on back to the barn. I kin git a lot a cawn shucked afore milkin' time.

MARVIN: I'm a-goin' that way myself. I'll go with you.

JOHN (*as* BARBARA *exits, with* MARVIN *starting to follow her*):
I reckon she kin make hit by herself, Marvin Hudgens. Reckon
she kin walk that fur alone.

MARVIN: But the path a free trail, John boy. I reckon I kin walk
hit if I wants.

(MARVIN *starts to swagger off, and* JOHN *dives for him.* MAR-
VIN *throws him to the ground.*)

MARVIN: Don't fergit what I showed you 'bout the choppin'.
Hit the long easy strokes that cut the most.

(*He strolls off, and* JOHN *half gets up as if to strike him with
lightning again, then stops. At length he gets up and goes
back to the log, where he picks up the axe and begins chopping
again. A* WITCH *appears and dances towards him.*)

WITCH: Witch boy!

(*The other* WITCH *reappears, laughing and calling to him.*)

WITCHES: Witch boy! Witch boy! Witch boy!

(*They laugh and dance around him, but he refuses to pay any
attention to them and goes on furiously chopping as the lights
fade.*)

Scene II

The scene is inside John's and Barbara's one-room cabin. BARBARA
*is lying in bed, asleep. At the foot of the bed is tied a knotted
sheet.* MRS. SUMMEY, *the midwife, comes across from outside
with a kettle, stopping to rearrange the bedclothes as she passes
the bed. She is singing.*

MRS. SUMMEY:
Up on Old Baldy all covered with snow,
I lost my true love fer courtin' too slow,
Oh, courtin' is pleasure, but partin' is grief,
And a falsehearted lover is worse than a thief.

Oh, if my lover is faithful, then I will be true,
But if he goes roamin' I'll go roamin' too.
He kin walk the world over, o'er land and o'er sea,
I'll be waitin' fer ever with someone else on my knee.
Oh, I wish I was an apple, a-hangin' on a tree,
And every time my true love passed he'd take a bite out of me.

(She puts the kettle on the stove as MRS. ALLEN *enters.)*

MRS. ALLEN: How is she?

MRS. SUMMEY: She are asleep.

MRS. ALLEN: How she take hit when you tole her?

MRS. SUMMEY. I ain't tole her yit. Better let her git her sleep out afore she knows.

MRS. ALLEN: John been here?

MRS. SUMMEY: Nary a sign. Nary a sign a that blackhaired witch.

MRS. ALLEN: He ain't no witch. Leastways we don't know for sartin.

MRS. SUMMEY: I got proof enough to make me shore. I been midwifin' from Hawg Back Holler to Chunky Gal fer nigh on fifteen year—ain't nothin' ever happen like this afore.

MRS. ALLEN: What you talkin' 'bout?

MRS. SUMMEY: Why, I'm talkin' 'bout her young un.

MRS. ALLEN: Lots a babies git born dead.

MRS. SUMMEY: This here weren't no baby.

MRS. ALLEN: What you mean? Lemme see it.

MRS. SUMMEY: Hit ain't here.

MRS. ALLEN: Ain't here? What you done to hit?

MRS. SUMMEY: Miz Bergen done tuck it off.

MRS. ALLEN: Well she hadn't oughter. Hit warn't no kin a hern.

MRS. SUMMEY: I tole her so!

MRS. ALLEN: You tole her to? Why?

MRS. SUMMEY: Hit jes' as well fer you you didn't git no chanst to see hit. Shore am glad hit warn't no grandchild a mine.

*(*MRS. BERGEN *crosses into the house.)*

MRS. BERGEN: I done what you tole me. Hit a-burnin' in the fire.

MRS. ALLEN: You mean you burned the baby?

MRS. BERGEN: Hit warn't no baby, Miz Allen. Hit were a witch.

MRS. ALLEN: A witch?

MRS. BERGEN: Ain't no baby ever looked like that. Hit were black all over and didn't have no face hardly, and hit arms was all twisted like the claws of a bat.

MRS. ALLEN: Like the claws of a bat!

MRS. SUMMEY: John a witch, Miz Allen. Ain't no doubt about hit. He a witch shore enough, and he done spelled he own wife.

BARBARA (*stirring weakly*): John? Whar John?

MRS. ALLEN: See, you done woke her. Woke her with yer yellin'.

BARBARA: Whar John, Maw? I wants John.

MRS. ALLEN: He be here right off, honey. They gone to git him.

BARBARA: Whar my baby, Maw? They wouldn't give hit to me.

MRS. ALLEN: Don't you worry 'bout that, child.

BARBARA: But I wants him, Maw. Whar is he? (MRS. ALLEN *turns away.*) Whar my baby?

MRS. ALLEN: He dead.

BARBARA (*beginning to cry softly*): Dead? My baby dead?

MRS. ALLEN: I'm sorry, honey. The Lord he give, and the Lord he take away.

BARBARA: But, Maw, I were real careful. I did jes' like they tole me. I pull on the sheet till the room go black with pain.

MRS. SUMMEY: Hit warn't no fault a yourn, child. Hit were the fruit a yer husband. You couldn't help what he done.

MRS. ALLEN: Hesh yore mouth!

MRS. SUMMEY: She got to know sometime.

BARBARA: What you mean, Miz Summey? Maw, what Miz Summey mean?

MRS. ALLEN: I tell you sometime, honey, when you strong enough to bear it.

BARBARA: I wanta know now, Maw, if hit got to do with John.

MRS. SUMMEY: Well, she gotta know some time, if she don't aready, so I reckon I'll tell her. Yore husband, he a witch.

BARBARA: No, he ain't! I know folks is a-sayin' so, but hit ain't true.

MRS. SUMMEY: He are a witch, and this here prove hit.

BARBARA: No he ain't! He ain't no witch!

MRS. SUMMEY: Then how come he give you a witch fer a child?

MRS. ALLEN: A witch fer a child.

MRS. BERGEN: Hit out thar a-burnin' now in the yard.

(BARBARA *screams and begins sobbing.*)

MRS. SUMMEY: Hit the only thing to do when you birth a witch. Hit can't have no funeral in no house a Gawd.

MRS. BERGEN: In no house a Gawd.

MR. ALLEN (*coming in*): Well, Maw, I hope you satisfied. This marryin' wasn't no ideer a mine.

MRS. ALLEN: How could I know she was a marryin' a witch?

MR. ALLEN: I coulda told you he were a witch, if you'd only jes' ast me.

BARBARA: He ain't no witch! He ain't no witch!

MR. ALLEN: Hesh up, gal. Course he a witch. And you gonna git outen the house afore hit too late.

MRS. ALLEN: You can't move her now, Paw. She jes' been in labor. If you take her outen this bed hit'll kill her shore.

MR. ALLEN: Well, she can't stay here, and that a fact a Jesus.

MRS. SUMMEY: Hit won't hurt nothin', as long as her husband ain't here.

MR. ALLEN: I knowed no good'd come from gittin' married in a general store.

MRS. ALLEN: The milk done spilt, Paw. Hit too late fer cryin'.

MR. ALLEN: Well hit ain't too late fer to take her home.

BARBARA: This here my home, Paw. I ain't a-goin' to leave hit.

MR. ALLEN: Then whar yer husband, gal?

MRS. BERGEN: I kin tell you whar he be. He out ridin' with the eagles. He out diggin' in the graveyard.

BARBARA: No, he ain't. He ain't no witch.

MRS. SUMMEY: Well, don't you fret too much, child. You jes' rest and git yer strength. You had a hard time in labor, and you done wore yerself plumb out.

(PREACHER HAGGLER *comes in.*)

HAGGLER: Howdy, brethren and sisters.

ALL: Howdy, Preacher Haggler.

HAGGLER: Jes' heard the news, so thought I'd stop to pray.

MRS. ALLEN: You a man a Gawd, Preacher Haggler.

HAGGLER: Well, Sister Allen, I looks after my flock. When they sick and afflicted, when they's sinned, and when they's strayed.

MRS. SUMMEY: Hit the Gawd's truth, Lord.

MRS. ALLEN: Preacher Haggler, what we gonna do? My gal she been witched, been married to a witch.

BARBARA: No, I ain't. He ain't no witch.

HAGGLER: Whenever trouble comes upon us, and we don't know what to do, nor which way to go, we got to turn to Jesus.

MRS. SUMMEY: Amen. Turn to Jesus.

HAGGLER: We got to turn to Jesus. He showed us the way.

MRS. SUMMEY: Yes, show us the way, Lord, show us the way.

HAGGLER: O Gawd, look down on this here woman. She a sinner, Gawd, she a sinner.

MR. ALLEN: Amen.

HAGGLER: She been follerin' after the lust a the flesh. She pleasured herself afore she were married. Gawd, she a sinner.

ALL: Amen.

HAGGLER: But Thou in Thy infinite mercy fergive her.

MRS. BERGEN: Fergive her, Lord, fergive her.

HAGGLER: She tuck herself a witch fer a husband, and Lord, he spelled her and he witched her, and she couldn't hep herself. But now he gone and left her.

BARBARA: He ain't left me! He come back.

HAGGLER: So show her what to do, Gawd, to git the sin outa her life.

MRS. ALLEN: Yes, show her what to do, Lord, show her what to do.

HAGGLER: The fires a the devil are ragin' 'round her, but she ain't got no sorrer and she can't repent.

MRS. BERGEN: She can't repent.

MR. ALLEN: She can't repent.

HAGGLER: Take her sin away, Lord, take hit outen her life. Cut hit outen her heart like a cutaway stone.

ALL: Like a cutaway stone, like a cutaway stone.

(JOHN *suddenly appears.*)

JOHN: What you all doin' here in my house?

BARBARA: John! I knowed you'd come back to me. I knowed hit.

HAGGLER: We been prayin' to Gawd to save this gal, this gal that you done witched.

JOHN: I ain't witched her! She my wife!

MRS. ALLEN: Whar you at, boy, while the gal's been in labor?

JOHN: I been outside. I been walkin' up by Old Baldy.

MR. ALLEN: That warn't no place to be while yer wife was beddin' yer own child. Maybe you'd like to know what come of yer child. Well, I kin tell you, witch boy. He a-burnin' in the yard. He a-burnin' with fire, for he were born a witch!

JOHN: Git outen my house! All a you, git out!

HAGGLER: We come to hep. That ain't no way to treat us.

JOHN: Git out, I say, if you know what good fer you.

MRS. SUMMEY: I'm a-goin', witch boy. Don't you spell me.

(*She goes out followed by* MRS. ALLEN *and* MRS. BERGEN.)

JOHN: Git on out thar, all of you. (HAGGLER *and* ALLEN *leave.*) And don't be hangin' 'round outside. (*He watches them go, then steps in that direction.*) What fer they burn my baby? What fer they do a thing ilke that?

BARBARA: They 'lowed hit a witch.

JOHN: They a-lyin'. Hit were our baby. Hit warn't no witch.

BARBARA: I wish you'd been here to tell 'em so.

JOHN: I were outside. I were walkin' on the mounting.

BARBARA: Why you leave me, John?

JOHN: I don't know! (*Pause.*) His jes' that sometimes bein' human's more'n I kin stand. I know hit what I wanta be, but sometimes I feel I jes' got to git away.

BARBARA: Git away from what?

JOHN: I can't explain, Barbara. You wouldn't understand. But sometimes after plowin' all day in the sun, I jes' gotta go somewhar alone when hit night—somewhar far off, whar hit dark and black. So I go to Old Baldy. Up thar on the mounting. I look at them stars, all them planets a-twistin' and changin' out thar in space. Then I know that this'n I'm standin' on, hit ain't so much, hit little, hit twistin' and changin' too. And I wanta be somethin' more'n jes' that! So I pretend that things is different, that I ain't the same as I am in the day.

BARBARA: What is hit you pretend, John?

JOHN: I can't tell you, Barbara. You wouldn't love me if I tole you.

BARBARA: No, perhaps you'd better not. Perhaps I know aready. Perhaps what all the others is sayin' is true.

JOHN: Sayin' 'bout what?

BARBARA: 'Bout the baby. But how could hit be a witch with us both humans?

JOHN (taking her in his arms): We both human now.

BARBARA: What you mean, now?

JOHN: I mean the next time we have a baby hit'll be a human fer shore.

BARBARA: Then hit true what they been sayin'. Hit true you a witch that first night we met, that night the moon went dark.

JOHN: That were afore the Conjur Woman changed me. I ain't a witch no more.

BARBARA: And are you changed fer allus?

JOHN: I reckon, if you want me.

BARBARA: You won't never change back, will you?

JOHN: That depend on you.

BARBARA: On me?

JOHN: Conjur Woman tole me I could be a human if you'd be faithful to me fer jes' one year.

BARBARA: I ain't never been with no one, not sinst I knowed you.

JOHN: I love you, Barbara Allen. (He kisses her.)

BARBARA: I love you, John.

(He gently settles her on the pillow, and she drifts off to sleep. He watches her a moment. Suddenly he leaps from the bed-side, stops and turns back to look at BARBARA. Then he drops his head in his hands and goes out into the yard.)

(*The* DARK WITCH *appears in the tree.*)

DARK WITCH: So you had a baby, witch boy!

JOHN: You ain't got no business here. This here ain't no place fer witches.

DARK WITCH: I see she a red head.

JOHN: She got copper hair. What you doin' here?

DARK WITCH: I was flyin' by to look at yore wife.

JOHN: Well you seen her now. You better git goin'.

(*The* FAIR WITCH *appears beside the* DARK WITCH.)

FAIR WITCH: John Human!

JOHN: What that to you?

(*By now he has backed up against the tree.*)

FAIR WITCH: Lonesome, ain't you?

DARK WITCH: All humans are. The minute you're a human you want somethin' lastin'.

FAIR WITCH: That's the reason they git married.

DARK WITCH: She can't ever know you.

FAIR WITCH: She can't ever understand.

JOHN: Leave me be!

FAIR WITCH: Miss the moonlight, don't you?

DARK WITCH: Moonlight's on the mounting.

FAIR WITCH: Feels so soft against my shoulders. I been up thar a-layin' in hit and a singin' to myself.

DARK WITCH: Yer eagle up thar too, boy. He gittin' lonesome.

FAIR WITCH: She ain't fer you, boy.

JOHN: I'm *human* now!

DARK WITCH: You can't ever hold her.

FAIR WITCH: She can't understand. Humans never know each other.

DARK WITCH: Never really find each other.

FAIR WITCH: Kiss her, but you're alone, boy. Kiss her, but you're lost.

JOHN: I ast you to leave me be!

DARK WITCH: You're astin' fer all time, boy, instead of jes' to-night.

FAIR WITCH: Three hundred years—don't ast fer more.

JOHN: What you want of me?

DARK WITCH: The earth's a-turnin', boy, to the night when Barbara leave you. Feel hit turnin'? Feel hit turnin'? (JOHN *buries his face in his hands.*) You'll be sorry, boy. (*She disappears.*)

FAIR WITCH: You'll be sorry! (*She disappears.*)

JOHN: Barbara! Barbara Allen (*He runs towards* BARBARA.) Barbara! Barbara Allen! (*He falls, sobbing, on the bed, his arms around* BARBARA.) Barbara! Barbara! Barbara Allen!

CURTAIN

Scene III

The mountain ridge, same as Act I, Scene I. The DARK WITCH *is sitting atop the rock and calls down.*

DARK WITCH: Conjur Man. Conjur Man.

(*The* CONJUR MAN *appears.*)

CONJUR MAN: What that?

DARK WITCH: I got some news fer you.

CONJUR MAN: Whar are you?

DARK WITCH: I'm here. Heard about the revival meetin' at the church to-night?

(*The* FAIR WITCH *appears on the rock.*)

CONJUR MAN: What you mean?

DARK WITCH: Witch boy gonna lost he bargain—bargain he made with you.

CONJUR MAN: Hit warn't no bargain a mine. Had nothin' to do with hit.

FAIR WITCH: He gonna lose he bargain and he be a witch agin.

CONJUR MAN: I reckon that'd please you.

DARK WITCH: I reckon.

CONJUR MAN: That don't mean you'll ever git him back. He'll still be in love with Barbara Allen.

DARK WITCH: Not after she untrue to him. Not after she been faithless with another man.

FAIR WITCH: She break the bargain, and he be a witch agin.

CONJUR MAN: But he still love Barbara. He still love Barbara Allen.

DARK WITCH: Not after she leave him. You fergit that he a human.

FAIR WITCH: He still a human till he turn back to a witch. And humans, they is differenr. Thar love can turn to hatin' when the gal untrue.

CONJUR MAN: And Barbara gonna leave him?

DARK WITCH: Hit the will a heaven.

FAIR WITCH: Yes, sir. Hit the will a heaven.

CONJUR MAN: I know hit ain't my business, but I do feel right sorry fer the boy, right sorry.

DARK WITCH: Well, hit'll be the best thing fer him.

FAIR WITCH: He better off with us.

CONJUR MAN: You ain't got him yit, witch gals.

FAIR WITCH: But we git what we goes after.

DARK WITCH: We never lose wunst we make up our mind.

CONJUR MAN: You seem mighty sartin.

FAIR WITCH: We are. Have you seen him sinst he been changed to a human?

CONJUR MAN: No, I ain't.

FAIR WITCH: Well, I reckon you'll git a chanst to soon enough. After church to-night you'll see him.

DARK WITCH: Shore. He be up here a-beggin' to git outen he bargain. He be up here to ast to stay down thar in the valley.

CONJUR MAN: No he won't neither. He made a bargain and he be true to he word.

DARK WITCH: You mighty shore a yer opinion.

CONJUR MAN: I reckon.

FAIR WITCH: How would you like a little bet that you wrong?

CONJUR MAN: I ain't averse to hit.

FAIR WITCH: If we lose, we promise to give up the witch boy.

CONJUR MAN: You won't git him anyway, but hit a bet.

DARK WITCH: And if we win, you got to promise to do somethin' fer us.

CONJUR MAN: What is hit you want?

DARK WITCH: The life a Barbara Allen.

CONJUR MAN: You plenty jealous, ain't you.

FAIR WITCH: We ain't got nothin' agin her, but we jes' as soon she dead.

CONJUR MAN: She live a long time, witch gals.

BOTH WITCHES: You backin' outen the bargain?

FAIR WITCH: Thought you said you was mighty shore what John boy would do.

CONJUR MAN: I am shore.

DARK WITCH: Then the bet still on?

CONJUR MAN: Hit still on.

FAIR WITCH (*running up on to the rock again*): Then you better git ready to change a man back to a witch!

(*The* CONJUR WOMAN *comes out of the cave and looks toward them, then goes off-stage.*)

CONJUR MAN: That ain't none a my doin's. I didn't change him, and hit ain' up to me to change him back. Asides, he ain't lost yit.

DARK WITCH (*as church bells begin ringing in the distance*): Hear the bells a-ringin'? They startin' the revival. Barbara git redemption, and John'll be a witch agin to-night!

(*She and the* FAIR WITCH *watch the valley from the rock, as the lights fade.*)

Scene IV

The scene is the interior of the Church of God in Buck Creek. A little left of center is the rostrum, and facing it are benches made of unfinished pine. Left of the rostrum is the mourner's bench and the choir loft, where the accordionist provides music. It is Sunday evening, and already the crowd has begun to gather. Those present, including HANK GUDGER, *on the mourners' bench, and* PREACHER HAGGLER, *are singing.*

GROUP: 'Tis the old time religion, 'Tis the old time religion. 'Tis the old time religion, It's good enough for me. It was good for our mothers, it was good for the Prophet Daniel, It was good for the Hebrew children, It will do when I am dying, It will take us all to heaven, etc.

HAGGLER (*welcoming arrivals*): Evenin', Sister Hattie. That a mighty fancy dress you're wearin'.

HATTIE (*shaking hands*): Why, Preacher Haggler! I ain't a fittin' sight to be seed, and that the diggin' fact. (*She joins the congregation.*)

HAGGLER: Evenin', Sister Greeny. How are you nohow?

GREENY: Evenin', Preacher. (*She sits.*) Good Evenin', Sister Summey. Glad to see you out.

MRS. SUMMEY: Evenin', Sister Greeny. I shore am heavy with trouble. Revival been going on now high on a week, and spirit ain't tuck Edna yit, not wunst, not nary a time.

MISS METCALF: Keep a-prayin', Sister, keep a-prayin'. Hit might could move her to-night.

MRS. SUMMEY: I shore Gawd hope hit do. (*To* EDNA, *beside her*) Git up thar, Edna Summey. Git up thar on the mourners' bench.

EDNA: I ain't got no sorrer yit. I'm a settin' here.

MRS. SUMMEY: Hank Gudger on the mourners' bench. He git redemption, reckon you kin too.

EDNA: I ain't been moved yit, Maw. I'm a-settin' here.

HAGGLER: Howdy, Miss Leafy.

LEAFY: Howdy, Preacher Haggler.

HAGGLER: Evenin', Brother Atkins.

ATKINS: Evenin', Preacher Haggler. Thar a right smart crowd here to-night.

(MRS. ALLEN, *pulling* BARBARA *along, comes in.*)

HAGGLER: Hit the will a Gawd. Lord carry He sheep right into the fold.

(BARBARA, *looking sullen and defiant, jerks her hand loose from* MRS. ALLEN'S *grip as they get to* HAGGLER.)

HAGGLER: Welcome, Sister Allen. Hit be some time sinst I saw yer daughter Barbara here.

MRS. ALLEN: Hit tuck a fight, Preacher Haggler, but the Lord won out.

HAGGLER: Praise He holy name!

GROUP: Amen, Lord, Amen.

MRS. BERGEN: Howdy, Miz Allen. So you got Barbara to come after all.

MRS. ALLEN: I drug her here. Hit the first time she been in the Church a Gawd sinst her confinement.

MRS. BERGEN: Well, hit'll do you good, Barbara. Give you peace and rest to your troubled soul.

BARBARA: My soul ain't troubled, Miz Bergen.

GREENY: Whar yer husband, gal?

(BARBARA *turns away.*)

MRS. ALLEN: He wouldn't come. We done tried everythin'. Look like nothin'd move him.

FLOYD: Said he warn't never puttin' foot in no house a Gawd.

HATTIE: He skeerd to, I reckon.

MRS. BERGEN: Witches can't stand the blood a the Lamb.

MRS. ALLEN: I reckon you right, thar, Sister Bergen.

MRS. SUMMEY: Is she still livin' with him?

MRS. ALLEN: Her paw done tried everythin' to git her to leave. Look like he done witched her fer shore.

MRS. BERGEN: Well, the Lord will find a way, sister. Jes' keep a-prayin'. The Lord will find a way.

MRS. ALLEN: Come on, Barbara. We's sittin' on the mourners' bench.

BARBARA: You kin if you want to, but I ain't.

MRS. ALLEN: You'll do like I say.

BARBARA: I won't git religion. Hit won't do no good.

(BARBARA *and* MRS. ALLEN *join* HANK *on the bench.*)

HAGGLER: Thar is still room on the mourners' bench, room for sinners that want to git saved.

SMELICUE (*coming in*): I'm a-comin', Preacher Haggler. I'm a-comin'. Spirit gonna move me to-night fer shore. (*He joins the rest on the mourners' bench.*)

HAGGLER: We will start the service with a hymn.

MRS. BERGEN: "As I wander," Preacher Haggler.

HAGGLER (*to the accordionist*): "As I Wander by that Lonesome Strand."

GROUP:

Take my hand, take my hand, and lead me to the promised land,

O Blessed Jesus, take my ha-ya-yand.

Take my hand, take my hand, and lead me through the sinkin' sand,

O Blessed Jesus, take my hand.

As I wander by that lonesome strand, there is a friend who waits fer me.

He will come and take me by the hand, he is the Christ of Calvaree-ee-ee.

This will be my feeble prayer, O Lordy, and I'll do the best I kin,

As I kneel in prayer, I hope to find you there,

O Blessed Jesus, take my hand.

HAGGLER: Amen, Lord, Amen. Take our hands and lead us to the land of Canaan. Thar is room fer another sinner on the mourners' bench. Who will come up? Who is heavy with trouble to-night?

(*He goes down among the congregation, pausing before* EDNA, *who still refuses to move.*)

Who wants the savin' graces the Lord Jesus Christ? Who want to lay the burden on the lap a Gawd?

MARVIN: I'm a sinner, Preacher Haggler, in the eyes a the Lord.

(*He comes down and goes over to the bench.*)

HAGGLER: Jes' repent, Brother Hudgens, and he wash hit away.

(HANK *and* SMELICUE *welcome* MARVIN *to the bench.*)

GROUP: Amen, Lord, Amen.

HAGGLER: One more song afore the prayer.

HATTIE: "Lonesome Valley."

HAGGLER (*as the accordionist sounds the key*): "You've got to Walk that Lonesome Valley."

GROUP:

> You've got to walk that lonesome valley,
> You've got to walk it by yerself,
> Ain't no one to go hit with you,
> You've got to walk it all alone.

SMELICUE:

> Thar's a crown a-waitin' fer me,
> When I tell this world good-bye,
> I will leave this vale a sorrer,
> For my mansion in the sky.

GROUP:

> You've got to walk, etc.

MISS METCALF:

> Thar were seven foolish virgins,
> Thar were seven wise and fair.

HAGGLER: It in the book, Sister!

MISS METCALF:

> Save yer oil fer yer lantern
> Watch yer step and you'll git thar.

GROUP:

> You've got to walk, etc.

HAGGLER: John the Baptist was a preacher.

SMELICUE: A preacher.

HAGGLER:

> Some folks say he was a Jew,
> Some folks say he was a Christian,
> But he was a Baptist too!

GROUP:

> You've got to walk, etc.

HAGGLER (*after the song*): Let us pray, O Gawd, we come here to-night with sorrer in our heart. They is sinners in our midst.

MRS. BERGEN: Hit the Gawd's truth, Lord.

HAGGLER: But we know who we kin turn to in this weary land. We know who we kin turn to who will lead us from our troubles, who will lift up the load with a pierced and bleedin' hand.

GROUP: With a pierced and bleedin' hand, with a pierced and bleedin' hand.

HAGGLER: We know who will lead us from the darkness of the night, from the valley of the shadow—

SMELICUE: From the fire a the devil—

HAGGLER: Though our sins be as scarlet, he will wash them white as snow.

GROUP: He will wash them white as snow, he will wash them white as snow.

HAGGLER: We ast fer mercy fer the sinners on the mourners' bench.

BENCH: O sweet Jesus, show us yer grace.

OTHERS: O sweet Jesus, shine yer holy face.

SMELICUE: Hep me, Jesus, take away my sin.

GROUP: Hep him, Jesus, see the trouble he in.

HAGGLER: Moan hit, brother, fer the Lord to hear.

MRS. BERGEN: Repent yer sin fer the Lord to hear.

GROUP: Save him by the grace a Gawd, Lord, save him by the grace a Gawd.

HAGGLER: Uncle Smelicue Jed, confess yer shame.

SMELICUE: My pockets so empty and my shoes so wore, that I had to take the cash from the register drawer.

GROUP: He had to take the cash from the register drawer, he had to take the cash from the register drawer!

SMELICUE: Hit were all a two dollar and seventy-five cent, but I bought me new shoes fer to walk in the light, fer to walk in the light a the Lord.

GROUP: He bought him new shoes fer to walk in the light, fer to walk in the light a the Lord.

SMELICUE: But now I'm sorry, and I repent.

MISS METCALF: He repent, Lord, he repent.

SMELICUE: So please fergive me and save me by grace.

GROUP: Save him by the grace a the heavenly Lamb, by the grace a the heavenly Lamb.

(*The accordionist sounds the key, and they all sing.*)

> He's washed in the blood and saved by grace,
> Saved from sin and shame and disgrace,
> He fell by the way, but he turned to Gawd to pray,
> And he's saved by the blood a the Lamb.

HAGGLER: Saved, saved. Go and sin no more.

SMELICUE (*rising*): I'm saved! Halleluiah, I'm saved!

(*He leaves the bench, amid congratulations, and joins the rest of the congregation.*)

HAGGLER: Thar is others on the mourners' bench. Who will be the next, Lord, who will be next? Does the spirit move you, Hank Gudger? Does the spirit move you to confess yer shame?

HANK: Hit ain't moved me yit.

MRS. SUMMEY: Git up thar with him, Edna Summey. Git up thar with him on the mourners' bench.

EDNA: I ain't got no sorrer. Not yit, I ain't.

MRS. SUMMEY: You can't git hit, gal, till you git on the bench.

SMELICUE: Git on the bench, Edna, git on the bench.

(EDNA, *however, sits firm.*)

HAGGLER: We will sing a hymn to hep convict Brother Gudger a his sin.

MRS. SUMMEY: "No, Never Alone."

HAGGLER (*to the accordionist*): "No, Never Alone."

> No, never alone,
> No, never alone,
> He promised never to leave me,
> Never to leave me alone;
> No, never alone,
> No, never alone,

He promised never to leave me,
Never to leave me alone.

(*During the chorus* HAGGLER *goes over to* HANK *and the two men can be seen arguing as to whether* HANK *is convinced. As the chorus ends* HAGGLER *leaves* HANK *and approaches the congregation.*)

HAGGLER: One more chorus and the Lord'll have him!

(*He goes back and kneels by* HANK, *who is beginning to get the spirit of salvation.*)

GROUP: No, never alone, etc.
(*On the last line* HANK *leaps from the bench and falls on his knees before the rostrum.*)

HANK: I'm convicted! I'm convicted!

GROUP: Halleluiah, he convicted a sin!

HAGGLER: Hank Gudger, confess yer shame.

HANK: I see the fires a hell come at me. I hear 'em roar. I feel 'em burn!

(EDNA *is watching him intently, reacting sympathetically.*)

HAGGLER: Tell yer sin to Jesus, to him you should turn.

GROUP: To him you should turn, to him you should turn.

HAGGLER: He put out the fire with he own red blood. Lay yer burden down, he wash hit with the Flood.

EDNA (*collapsing*): The spirit done tuck hold! I got sorrer and shame!

MRS. SUMMEY: Praise be to Gawd, my daughter repent!

HAGGLER: Come on down, Sister Summey, to the mourners' bench.

EDNA (*coming to join* HANK): I'm a-comin', Lord, I'm a-comin'.

HAGGLER: Continue, Brother Gudger. Tell the Lord yer shame.

EDNA: Hit my shame, too. Hit my shame too.

MISS METCALF: Praise the Lamb a Gawd, they's shamed to-gether!

HANK: We was in the barn, a-shuckin' dry corn.

EDNA: Cawn shucks soft, cawn shucks warm.

HANK: Her breast so firm and full and high, then we pleasured ourselves in the barn.

GROUP: They pleasured tharselves in the barn. Lord, they pleasured tharselves in the barn.

EDNA: We pleasured ourselves fer an hour and a quarter. We pleasured ourselves till hit milkin' time.

GROUP: Milkin' time, milkin' time.

HANK: But now we sorry, and we repent.

MRS. SUMMEY: They repent, Lord, they repent.

EDNA: So please fergive us and save us by grace.

GROUP: Save 'em by the grace a the heavenly Lamb, by the grace a the heavenly Lamb.

(*The accordionist leads off, and they sing.*)

> They's washed in the blood and saved by grace.
> Saved from sin and shame and disgrace.
> They fell by the way, but they turned to Gawd to pray,
> And they's saved by the blood a the Lamb!

HAGGLER: Saved, saved. Go and sin no more.

(HANK *and* EDNA *get up, hand in hand, and are congratulated by the congregation.* MRS. SUMMEY *pulls their hands apart.*)

MRS. ALLEN: Oh Gawd, save my child.

HAGGLER: Sister Allen, what is yer sorrer?

MRS. ALLEN: I got a daughter, Lord, who strayed from the path, but she got no shame and she won't repent.

HAGGLER: Lay yer burden on the Lord, He understand.

MRS. ALLEN: I brung up Barbara in the ways a Gawd, but a witch boy spelled her, and tuck her soul away.

MR. ALLEN: That's the Lord's truth. She been witched.

MRS. ALLEN: She bedded he child, but she bore him a witch, and we had to burn hit with fire in the yard.

GROUP: They had to burn hit with fire in the yard.

MRS. ALLEN: But she won't leave the witch boy. She live in the house. So take away the spell, Gawd, and save my child.

HAGGLER: The Lord'll unspell her in He own way. Jes' listen fer the voice a the Lord.

BARBARA (*who up to now has sat in stony defiance, refusing to take part in any of the service*): He might could have spelled me, but I don't care! (*She rises and faces the congregation.*)

GROUP: She witched fer shore, she witched fer shore.

BARBARA (*confronting them*): He wunst were a witch, but he ain't no more! Conjur Woman change him to a man.

HAGGLER: Wunst you're a witch you can't git changed. Thar ain't no changin' a witch to a man.

GROUP: That right, Lord, thar ain't no changin'.

BARBARA: Conjur Woman change him, change him fer shore.

HAGGLER: What he have to do to git changed?

BARBARA: Hit warn't jes' him. I have to be faithful to him fer a year. And the year up to-night!

GROUP: Hit ain't up yit. Hit ain't up yit.

HAGGLER: And if you ain't, what happen then?

BARBARA: Then he change back to a witch. But thar ain't no fear fer that. I'll keep my promise. I'll be true.

HAGGLER: The Lord He speakin' in a mighty voice. The Lord He tellin' me what to do!

MRS. ALLEN: What He say, Preacher Haggler? What He say?

HAGGLER: Barbara Allen, you a handmaiden a Gawd. You got to hep this valley and rid us of a witch.

ALL: A witch.

BARBARA: But he ain't no witch. He a man!

HAGGLER: He change back to a witch, and then he leave us be. You gotta break the spell and change him back.

BARBARA: But I promised him I'd be true!

HAGGLER: The Lord He talkin', Barbara Allen. Listen to He voice tell you what to do. You been walkin' after yer own way, walkin' in the valley a the shadow a darkness;

BARBARA: John! I need John! (*She looks about her, frightened.*)

MRS. ALLEN: He can't hep you now, gal.

BARBARA: He hep me if I find him.

(*She starts out of the church, but* MR. ALLEN *rises in her path.*)

MR. ALLEN: He don't love you no more, gal.

HAGGLER: You need the love a Gawd.

BARBARA: John still love me!

(*She backs up before* ALLEN *and several others who have risen.*)

MRS. BERGEN: Then how come he give you a witch fer a child?

(BARBARA *buries her face in her hands.*)

MARVIN: And why ain't he with you?

HAGGLER: He ain't here at church.

ALL: He ain't here at church.

BARBARA: He can't come to church.

GROUP: Hit cause he a witch, hit cause he a witch!

(BARBARA, *in evident distress, turns to the rostrum.*)

BARBARA: Oh, Preacher Haggler, what kin I do?

HAGGLER: You can't go agin the will a Gawd. The Lord He speakin' in a mighty voice.

MARVIN: Preacher Haggler! Preacher Haggler! I come here tonight to repent a my sin, but the Lord He tell me hit ain't no sin.

GROUP: Ain't no sin. Ain't no sin.

MARVIN (*as* BARBARA *watches in growing horror*): I come here to repent a sin a lust. I been lustin' after a married woman, lustin' fer the flesh a Barbara Allen. But the Lord He tell me hit ain't no sin!

GROUP: Ain't no sin. Ain't no sin.

BARBARA (*rushing toward the door*): John! John.

HAGGLER (*as several worshippers bar her way and force her back to the center*): Git on yer knees, git and hear the voice a the Lord.

GROUP: Git on yer knees, git on yer knees, git on yer knees and git washed in the blood.

(BARBARA *finds herself trapped by the congregation, who surround her. She turns one way and another, but cannot find an opening for escape.*)

HAGGLER: Show her, Gawd, the fruit a her sin!

GROUP: Hep her, Gawd, see the trouble she in!

(BARBARA *covers her face with her hands, swaying from side to side.*)

HAGGLER: Listen to the Lord, He ease yer pain, wash away yer sin like the mountain rain.

GROUP: Like the mountain rain, like the mountain rain.

HAGGLER: Git on yer knees and confess yer shame.

BARBARA (*crying*): What kin I do? What kin I do?

HAGGLER: Ast the hep a Gawd, He see you through.

GROUP: Tell yer sin to Gawd He's shore to hear.

HAGGLER: Wash her in the blood a the Lamb, Lord.

GROUP: Wash her in the blood a the Lamb!

(BARBARA *falls to her knees.*)

BARBARA: Oh, my Jesus, take my sin away!

GROUP: Halleluiah, Lord, she startin' to pray!

HAGGLER: Moan hit, sister, fer the Lord to hear. He died on the cross to save you from sin. Marvin's here to hep you, jes' turn to him.

MARVIN (*coming down to* BARBARA, *who is sobbing*): That right, Barbara, hit the will a Gawd.

(*He picks her up and holds her against him despite her attempts to make him release her.*)

GROUP: It the will a Gawd! The will a Gawd!

MARVIN: Feel my arms around you. They fer comfort and joy.

BARBARA: John! . . . John!

GROUP (*as* MARVIN *and* BARBARA *sink to the floor*): Halleluiah, Lord, she saved by the grace, she saved by the grace a the heavenly Lamb, by the grace a the heavenly Lamb.

(*Through the last line* JOHN'S *voice is heard calling.*)

JOHN: Barbara! Barbara Allen.

BLACKOUT

Scene V

The scene is the mountain ridge again. The DARK WITCH *and the* FAIR WITCH *are reclining on the rock. Offstage* BARBARA *is heard calling.*

BARBARA: John! John! (*She comes in and sits a moment to rest.*) John! (*She gets up and starts across, weeping and evidently tired.*) John!

DARK WITCH: What the matter, gal?

BARBARA (*looking around for the invisible speaker*): Oh!

FAIR WITCH: Is you skeerd, gal?

BARBARA: Who you?

DARK WITCH: We know you, gal.

FAIR WITCH: Her name Barbara.

(BARBARA, *unable to see them, sits on the edge of the rock nearest the sound.*)

BARBARA: You witches, ain't you?

DARK WITCH: I reckon.

BARBARA: You ain't seed John! You ain't seed my husband?

DARK WITCH: What the matter gal? He left you?

BARBARA: He warn't thar when I come home to-night. I gotta find him.

FAIR WITCH: You'll never find him. He gone forever.

BARBARA: But I gotta see him. I gotta explain.

DARK WITCH: Ain't no explainin' the will a heaven.

FAIR WITCH: Ain't no explainin' that to a witch.

BARBARA: John ain't no witch. He a human.

FAIR WITCH: You mighty shore.

BARBARA: He wouldn't change hisself back to a witch without first tellin' me goodbye.

DARK WITCH: He left you, gal. He gone forever.

BARBARA: I gotta see him. Can't you tell me? Can't you tell me whar he be?

DARK WITCH: He don't wanta see you, gal.

FAIR WITCH: He don't wanta see you, after to-night.

BARBARA: I couldn't help it. They made me do hit.

DARK WITCH: But you broke yer promise, and he lost he bargain. The Conjur Woman gonna make him pay.

BARBARA: Ain't thar nothin' I kin do to stop hit?

DARK WITCH: Ain't nothin'.

FAIR WITCH: You better git on back down to the valley.

BARBARA: No, John here somewhar, and I'll find him. (*She gets up and starts off.*) John! John!

DARK WITCH (*as she disappears*): You'll never find him, gal.

FAIR WITCH: He gone forever. He done left the valley.

DARK WITCH: The valley so low.

FAIR WITCH: Hang yer head low, gal.

DARK WITCH: Feel the wind blow.

FAIR WITCH: Feel the wind blowin'.

DARK WITCH: Feel the wind blow.

(*The* CONJUR MAN *looms out of the darkness.*)

CONJUR MAN: You still up thar?

DARK WITCH: We kin wait ferever to git our way.

CONJUR MAN: Who that gal that jes' went by?

DARK WITCH: That Barbara Allen. She come here lookin' fer John.

FAIR WITCH: Pore gal. She be daid afore tomorrer.

DARK WITCH: She be daid afore hit light.

CONJUR MAN: You mighty sartin.

DARK WITCH: Ain't never lost a bet.

FAIR WITCH: Don't make 'em lest we sartin.

CONJUR MAN: Well, we'll see. We'll wait and see.

(*The* FAIR WITCH *suddenly moves back against the rock, for over the peak* JOHN *laboriously climbs.*)

JOHN: Whar the—— (*He sees the* WITCHES *and stops, then sees the* CONJUR MAN *below.*) Whar the Conjur Woman?

CONJUR MAN: What the matter?

JOHN (*climbing down clumsily*): I got to see the Conjur Woman.

CONJUR MAN: Livin' in the valley I reckon warn't so easy, warn't so easy as ridin' on an eagle in the night. I done all I could to tell you, but you wouldn't listen. And now you sorry.

JOHN: No, I ain't. I ain't sorry. But I gotta see the Conjur Woman. I gotta ast her somethin'.

CONJUR MAN: You better not ast her nothin'. You better leave her be.

JOHN: Then she change me back to a witch.

CONJUR MAN: What fer?

JOHN: Cause I lost our bargain.

FAIR WITCH: So Barbara been off with another man.

(*She and the* DARK WITCH *laugh.*)

JOHN: You keep outen this.

CONJUR MAN: Then I reckon you mad at her.

JOHN: I ain't mad at her. I couldn't git mad at Barbara Allen.

CONJUR MAN: Then you still love her?

JOHN: I'll allus love her.

CONJUR MAN: Even when you change back to a witch?

JOHN: Even then, I reckon.

DARK WITCH: Suppose she git married to someone else?

JOHN: What you got to do with this?

DARK WITCH: I'm waitin' fer somethin' you gonna do.

JOHN: I ain't doin' nothin' that you got to do with.

CONJUR MAN: Let me warn you, witch boy——

FAIR WITCH: You can't tell him, Conjur Man. That breakin' our bargain.

JOHN: Bargain? What bargain? Tell me, Conjur Man.

CONJUR MAN: Leave here, John, and don't never come back.

JOHN: But I got to see the Conjur Woman. I got to ast her somethin'.

CONJUR MAN: Don't do hit, witch boy. I'm a warnin' you.

JOHN: I don't want yore warnin'. You told me not to be a human. You were agin hit all along.

CONJUR MAN: Hit were fer yer good I tole you.

CONJUR WOMAN (*off-stage*): Is that you, John?

(*She comes into view.*)

JOHN (*running toward her*): Conjur Woman!

CONJUR WOMAN: I were expectin' you here to-night. I'm glad to see you kept yer promise.

JOHN: Hit about that I come to see you.

DARK WITCH: Go on, ast her!

CONJUR MAN (*warningly*): John!

JOHN: I want you to give me another chanst——

CONJUR MAN: No, John, wait!

JOHN: Let me be a human jes' a little while longer!

FAIR WITCH: We've won!

DARK WITCH: See, Conjur Man. We've won!

JOHN: What you talkin' about?

DARK WITCH: We've won the life a Barbara Allen.

JOHN: How come?

DARK WITCH: We knowed you'd want to go back on yer promise. We bet the Conjur Man you would. We've won her life,
and we wants to be paid afore hit mornin'.

JOHN (*leaping up the rock to face her*): What hit to you to have
Barbara's life?

FAIR WITCH: We ain't jes' winnin' her life. We bringin' you
back. Bringin' you back to the moonlight, and us.

JOHN: No, you ain't.

DARK WITCH: To the moonlight, and us.

JOHN: That ain't fer me.

FAIR WITCH: Remember, John boy, can't you remember? Remember those nights up thar in the sky, you in my arms on
the screamin' wind—how free we all was then. Can't you remember?

JOHN: But hit's over. Hit's finished!

DARK WITCH: Hit's jes' the beginnin'. When you a witch agin,
you'll see things different.

JOHN: But I'll allus remember, and I'll allus love her.

FAIR WITCH: You'll change yore mind. (*She disappears over the
rock.*)

DARK WITCH: We'll be a-waitin'. (*She too disappears.*)

JOHN: If Barbara die, let me die with her.

CONJUR MAN: You a witch, and you gotta live out yer time.

CONJUR WOMAN: Are you ready, John boy, ready fer the
changin'? Hit time to be turned back to a witch.

JOHN: Give me jes' a little longer.

CONJUR WOMAN: The year up to-night. She got to be dead
afore the new day.

JOHN: Don't let her see me wunst I'm a witch.

CONJUR MAN (*exits into cave*): You turn to a witch the minute
she die.

JOHN: I'll see her agin. I'll fly to her on my eagle. (*He starts off.*)

CONJUR WOMAN: Not yit you can't fly. You still a human.

BARBARA (*offstage*): John!

CONJUR WOMAN: The moon, witch boy! When the moon break through the clouds, you'll be a witch agin. (*She too vanishes in the blackness.*)

BARBARA (*as she comes onstage*): John!

(*She sees him and stops.*)

John.

JOHN: We met afore, Barbara Allen. The night the wind came up and the moon went dark. Remember?

BARBARA: I remember.

JOHN: And thar ain't no moon to-night.

BARBARA: And thar a wind.

JOHN: Remember yer ballad? You said hit wouldn't be sad. You allus like the gay ones best.

BARBARA: I'm sorry. I'm sorry I spiled the ballad.

JOHN: Hit ain't spiled. Hit jes' ends sad. What matters is the singin', and hit still a good song.

BARBARA: All about a witch boy who tried to be human.

JOHN: And the gal he witched, who was untrue.

BARBARA: I couldn't hep it. They made me do hit. They said hit were the will a Gawd.

JOHN: The will of Gawd. I don't know that. I ain't no Christian.

BARBARA: Take me with you, John, take me with you. Hit don't matter whar you go, hit don't matter how fur hit be. Take me out a the valley. I want to be with you.

JOHN: Hit wouldn't hep none. Not now hit won't.

BARBARA: What you mean, John?

JOHN: You gotta die, Barbara Allen.

BARBARA: I gotta die?

JOHN: Jes' like the ballad, the song you was singin'. Someone gotta die when the song ends sad.

BARBARA: Ain't thar nothin' I kin do to change hit?

JOHN: Ain't nothin' now. Song almost sung.

BARBARA: Not yit. Hit ain't time yit.

JOHN: We ain't got much longer. When the moon breaks through I'll be a witch agin.

BARBARA: Promise you'll find me. Promise you'll come.

JOHN: I can't promise that. A witch got no soul. Three hundred years, then jes' fog on the mountain.

BARBARA: Ain't nothin' else?

JOHN: Ain't nothin' else.

BARBARA (*taking off her wedding ring*): Take my ring, John, the ring you gave me. Hit got a green stone that shine in the dark.

JOHN: Our weddin' ring, from the day we was married. (*He looks at the ring.*)

BARBARA: Promise you'll wear hit, you'll wear hit always.

JOHN: Somethin' from the time when I warn't no witch, from the days I worked in the burnin' sun, from the nights I held you here in my arms. (*He takes her in his arms.*) and we talked of the baby we was gonna have. We said he'd have blue eyes.

BARBARA: Fergive me, John. Fergive me.

JOHN: Hit the last night I kin look at you jes' like you are now, the last time I kin reach out and take yer hand, the last time I kin hold you in my arms and feel yer breath warm against my cheek——

BARBARA (*startled*): What that I hear, John? High overhead, like the flappin' a wings?

JOHN: Hit my eagle! He comin' with the moonlight. He comin' down to git me!

BARBARA: Hit come so quick! Hit come so quick!

JOHN: The moon! The moon, Barbara! I kin almost see hit.

BARBARA: I'm skeerd! I'm skeerd a dyin'. (*She almost falls.*)

JOHN: Barbara! (*He kisses her.*)

BARBARA (*faintly*): Hold me, John.

JOHN (*he picks her up in his arms and gradually her head and arms relax and hang lifeless. Slowly he carries her over to a ledge of the rock and gently puts her down. The moon begins to show through the clouds*): Hit the end a the singin'. Ain't nothin' left. None a the words.

(*Suddenly, as the moonl:ght brightens around him his body stiffens and with a wild alertness he looks slowly around him. As he sees the moon, now full and bright, he leaps away from* BARBARA, *unaware of her.*)

DARK WITCH (*running in*): Witch boy. (*She catches his hand.*)

FAIR WITCH (*catching the other hand*): We come fer you, witch boy.

DARK WITCH: Yer eagle waitin' fer you. He here to take you back.

(*The three start offstage,* JOHN *still fascinated by the moon. He stops to gaze at it again and the* WITCHES *notice the ring.*)

DARK WITCH: Whar you git that ring, boy?

FAIR WITCH: Hit got a green stone, and hit shine in the dark.

(JOHN *slips the ring off and looks at it a moment.*)

JOHN: I got hit—I got hit from the grave a Agnes Riddle. I cut it off the finger of her cold, dead hand.

(*The three laugh.*)

FAIR WITCH: Let me wear hit, witch boy. Let me keep hit fer you.

(JOHN *holds it a moment as if to refuse, then hands it to her.*)

JOHN: All right, I reckon.

(*The* FAIR WITCH *runs offstage.*)

DARK WITCH (*starting off after her*): Come, witch boy. Time to go. (*She goes offstage.*)

(JOHN *starts to follow, then again looks at the moon.*)

JOHN: Look at the moon!

(*Turning back, he sees* BARBARA *lying on the rocks. He runs over to her. Slowly he picks up her hair and lets it fall through his fingers. Turning quickly, he pushes her body with his foot.*)

DARK WITCH (*offstage*): John

FAIR WITCH (*offstage*): Witch boy!

(*The scream of the eagle is heard.* JOHN *runs toward it.*)

CURTAIN

SONGS FROM *DARK OF THE MOON*
LIFE'S OTHER SIDE

A PURE GAL left her mother----- She was
fur a--way from home--- She walk'd the
streets of Ashe-ville--- So cold and so a--
lone---- A man he came up----
to her--- And he took her-- by the arm---
---- And said "Now I'll be good to you and
see you-- have no harm-----" He took her--
down a back street---- In--to a house of
sin--- And once that pore girl went in--side She

nev-er come out a---gain--- Just a

pitcher from life's oth-er side---- Some

bo-dy that fell by the way---- A

lite has gone out with the TIDE the

tide-- thee might have been hap-py some

day Some day--- Some poor old mother-- at

home a---lone ---- wait-in' and

watchin' in vain---- Wait-in' to

hear-from a loved one so dear- Just a

pitch-er from life's other side ----

THE OLD RELIGION

'Tis the old time religion, 'Tis the

old time religion 'Tis the

old time religion, It's good e-nough for me

NO NEVER ALONE

RELIGIOSO

No nev-er a---lone ----- No nev-er a--

lone -- He prom-ised nev-er to leave -- me

Nev-er to leave me a--lone ---- No, nev-er a--

lone -----No, nev-er a - lone -- He promised never to

leave ---me Nev-er to leave me a - lone ----

LONESOME VALLEY

— You got to   walk --- that lone some

val - ley --- You got to walk --- it by your

self Ain't no one --- to go it with you -- You got to

walk - it all a--lone John the Bap -- tist was a

preacher Some folks say --- he was a

Jew, Some folks say -- he was a Christian But he

was --- a Baptist   too ---

DOWN IN THE VALLEY

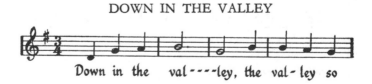

Down in the   val ----ley, the val - ley so

low - - - - - - - - Hang your head low, dear

Feel the wind blow - - - - - - - - - - -

THERE IS A FRIEND

As I wander by that lonesome strand There is a

friend who waits for me He will come and take me

by the hand He is the Christ of Cal--ver -

ee - - - - - This will be my feeble prayer O Lordy and I'll

do the best I can As I kneel in pray'r I

hope to find there O blessed Jesus Take my

hand - - Take my hand take my hand and lead me

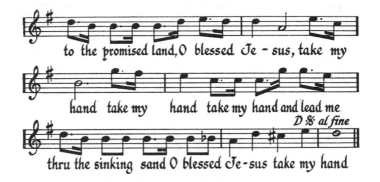

to the promised land, O blessed Je - sus, take my

hand   take my   hand   take my hand and lead me

D %. al fine

thru the sinking sand O blessed Je-sus take my hand

SMOKEY MOUNTAIN GAL

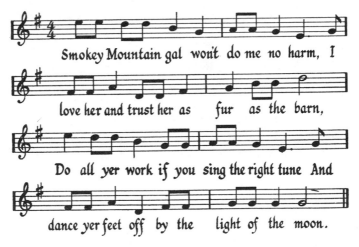

Smokey Mountain gal won't do me no harm, I

love her and trust her as   fur   as the barn,

Do all yer work if you sing the right tune And

dance yer feet off by the   light of the moon.